Theocrat

Theocrat

Hayden Hart

HYPATIA
PRESS

Published by Hypatia Press in the United Kingdom in 2023

ISBN: 978-1-83919-527-3

www.hypatiapress.org

Dedicated to the memory of Dorothy "Dot" Hart, for reading with me throughout my childhood.

Chapter 1

Reggie had chosen me to witness his execution. His family and the majority of his friends had publicly denounced him shortly after his face began dominating the news. I assumed that his ostracization had forced him to turn to his colleagues to fill the position. I had denounced him as well, but my allegiance to the State motivated me to attend regardless. Considering his newfound distrust of the Visryan government, he likely did not consider opting out of having a witness present. Reggie had been absent from work for a week or so, and requests for information leading to his arrest filled every other regional broadcast. His wanted posters covered every rec-center bulletin board within one-hundred miles, and warnings about the potentially dangerous heretic echoed through every public train car. Had they been able to arrest him sooner, the populace would have never known that a crime had been committed.

The other witnesses were to be randomly selected by the government; this transparency was intended to guarantee a humane execution. For this service, each witness was rewarded twenty-five Visryan dollars, roughly enough to eat out by oneself, and the pride of having assisted the State. After filling out a form, I was escorted along with the other witnesses to a waiting room connected to the execution chamber. Everyone chose seats far apart from one another. Watching someone die did not lend itself to conversation. Buzzing fluorescent lights drowned out everyone's nervous breathing. The woman across the room's face was obscured by the shadows cast by her bangs. She stared down at the scuffed linoleum tile, distracting herself by poking the floor's imperfections with her foot. The empty-looking man sitting a few chairs down from her watched a flickering light in the corner of the room. Every few minutes, he scratched the stubble on his face and rubbed his sunken-in eyes. The lighting accentuated his every wrinkle. He looked like a propped-up corpse. I wanted to turn around and watch the other witnesses, but the people sitting behind me would not have appreciated my invasive glances.

I invested the rest of my time in the digital clock over the steel double doors that led to the execution chamber. Reggie was to be killed at half past two, fifteen minutes after the witnesses were to be let in. A door in the corner rattled on its hinges while guards on the other side fidgeted with an endless litany of latches and locks before finally opening. It slammed against the already-chipped walls and revealed a portly, balding man with over a dozen medals obscuring his drab officer uniform. He was standing between unadorned, presumably lower-level employees.

"My name is Walden Matthews, and I work for the Relis branch of the Department of the Interior. I will be presiding over the execution and am in charge of directing the witnesses." He shuffled to the double doors and flung them open, wiping some sweat from his forehead before continuing. "Please enter the room and remain silent for the duration of the event. Any questions before proceeding?"

The witnesses exchanged a few quick glances with one another but remained silent. Walden stood at the door and waited for us to acclimate to our surroundings. The chamber itself was a cramped concrete coffin. A single row of twelve chairs facing a window looking into the chamber three feet away lined the back wall. One by one, we slid into our seats and awaited further instruction. The sickly green light spilling in from the chamber illuminated our decrepit room. Cobwebs filled with long-dead insect exoskeletons hung down from the corners of the chamber window. Small streams of murky moisture seeped through splintering cracks in the wall. The corpse-like man mumbled invectives as did several others as they took their seats.

"I thought this was gonna be different, like we were getting paid to walk in, get this thing done, and walk out with some cash. Why do they gotta make it so bad?" said the man sitting in the far corner.

I narrowed my eyes at him as did a few others. Such an outburst at a member of the Department of the Interior would have been unacceptable in private, let alone while they were on duty. Walden, seemingly unbothered, ignored the man and cleared his throat with impressive force to regain everyone's attention.

"Is there a Marlow Wilson here?" He leaned into the room, his gut nearly smothering the woman sitting closest to the door. I raised my hand.

"Yes, sir."

He nodded and pulled a crumpled piece of paper out of his uniform's front pocket.

"Do you swear on your eternal life that, if you are asked to do so, you will report today's events accurately to the best of your ability?"

"Yes, sir."

He scanned the page for a moment, having evidently lost his place.

"Your presence here fulfills the convict's right to have a witness of his choice present. Thank you for your cooperation." He backed out of the room and closed the doors, leaving us alone with each other in the chamber.

Aside from it being washed-out by green light, the other room was similar to ours. It was a bit larger, with a rusty, cracked control panel bolted to the wall. The same cobweb hammocks hung from its corners accentuated by the same cracks. I heard the familiar fumbling with locks and latches in the chamber somewhat muffled by the window in front of me. The chamber door opened towards the window, preventing us from seeing those entering. I heard a series of frustrated groans followed by a thud that nearly unhinged the door. A moment later, I finally saw a bruised and bloody Reggie.

The Reggie I had known was a healthy man in his late thirties. He was fairly tall and talkative with an exceptionally manicured beard, but these traits were nowhere to be found. Two guards dragged in a hunched-over, deflated corpse. My colleague had been reduced to a shivering anemic husk. They had forced him to shave his beard, a necessary measure for the State's prison face-recognition software to function properly. His lips quivered as he stared at me through the glass. I assumed that he was trying to communicate with me, but his mouthed words were indecipherable. The guards propped him up against the center of the back wall and gave him a crutch with which to steady himself. Presumably satisfied with the setting, Walden marched in and took his place in front of Reggie. He motioned to one of the guards who pressed a few buttons on the control panel.

"We will now proceed with the execution of Reginald Finster for the crimes of deliberately disseminating false information, transport of contraband across regional borders, and heresy." His voice crackled through speakers hidden above the chamber window. "I will now read the convict's final statement aloud."

A guard handed him a single piece of paper from a folder and excused himself from the room. This struck me as a strange departure from the norm. Reggie and I had worked together for the Department of Public Spending. Our jobs consisted mainly of identifying and eliminating inefficiencies in State spending. A few years earlier, someone in our department had been tasked with reducing waste in maintaining the rights of the convicted, and they found that, among those who were to be executed, the government was wasting millions on preventing tampering with convicts' written statements. For this reason, it became official policy to require all final statements to be spoken aloud. Reggie looked into my eyes and nodded as Walden cleared his throat.

"I would like to offer my sincerest apologies to my family and countrymen for the immoral and unlawful acts I have committed. My misdeeds have put the safety of not only you but also countless future generations in jeopardy. It is my hope that, by confessing my crimes, the State may have mercy on my soul and allow me to join you once again in the next life." Walden then stuffed the paper into his pocket.

After finishing, Walden took a moment to gauge the witnesses. Everyone looked unphased by the cookie-cutter last words. I struggled to contort my surprised expression into one of somber respect. He caught his breath and spoke again.

"We will now carry out the execution."

He and one of the guards exited the room, leaving one to attend to Reggie. He had not written that final statement. A deliberately constructed process had been entirely ignored by the agency most trusted to protect it! Not until the final statement was to be read did he make eye contact. They may have elected to use a thoroughly vetted, prewritten statement to avoid letting him blurt out classified information, but the standard-issue message Walden read was, I suspected, entirely fraudulent.

A series of metal clacks interrupted my thought process. The guard left behind to watch Reggie was replaced by two men sporting rifles. One of the men stood in the near left corner of the chamber with his back to the witnesses. The other man ambled to the opposite side, alternating between staring at us and Reggie, and took the right corner near the control panel. The men simultaneously shouldered their guns and took aim. The man on the right began counting down from ten, but Reggie seemed uninterested. His eyes followed a roach climbing across the inside of the chamber window. A convict usually used this moment to offer a brief prayer to Vexrus in the hope of being spared an eternity of non-existence, but he seemed to have accepted his fate. The man on the left looked to his partner and raised an eyebrow. His partner shrugged as the countdown concluded. Both men fired two three-round bursts into Reggie's torso. His ribcage splattered open, and he fell face down on the concrete. In an instant, he had been reduced to a pulsating pile of shredded viscera. A stream of his blood ran to a well-hidden drain just below the window.

"This is sick! Why do they make people watch this?!" the irreverent man who spoke out earlier exclaimed.

I considered jumping to the Department of the Interior's defense by explaining why the State chose a cheap, instant, undignified death over an overcomplicated ceremonial one, but decided that it would have been distasteful. Walden strutted in and crackled over the speaker once again with a flurry of legal jargon, but I was not listening. I stared at Reggie's corpse until I was instructed to leave. He had been my friend and colleague for years. Now he was gone. We each signed a form and were freed from our musty box. Shortly after the doors behind us slammed shut, underpaid employees would haul Reggie away by the bucketful and rinse what they could not carry down the drain. Visryan did not waste resources on burying the dead; instead, it tossed them into an incinerator.

At work the following day, I sat beside an empty chair and sloughed through a workload meant for two people. The State had already riffled through his desk and removed anything of note. If it were not for the torn synthetic leather on the arms of his desk chair, there would be no evidence of Reggie having ever existed. Aside from rumors circulating around the office, the world had washed its hands of him and moved on leaving only a well-used desk chair. I reclined in the light rays beaming through the blinds in our office.

Regardless of where he was now, both he and I were better off outside of that dungeon. The false final statement still bothered me. I was intimately familiar with the ins and outs of Visryan's public policy, and what I had witnessed was unacceptable. I did hold the Department of the Interior in fairly high regard, however, and was hesitant to suspect any sort of foul play. At any rate, if I were to mention this to the authorities, I needed to be certain that his executioners did not have a logical reason for why his rights were subverted. I would have hated for such a respected institution to think of me as an adversary. If I could analyze the banned materials he had supposedly plotted to distribute, I could likely solve the mystery and move on.

A message from my superior flashed across my computer screen, reminding me of an impending deadline and pulling me from my thoughts. I had nearly completed a project that Reggie and I had begun before his disappearance. We were tasked with finding a cheap way to manufacture copies of *The Book of Vexrus* overseas without worsening relations with the foreigners. We had secured land for a papermill and were finishing negotiations with local merchants for bulk leather purchases. I suggested that they should bind the books with something cheaper, but the State refused, asserting that "such a sacred book deserves a proper binding."

Projects involving State-sponsored conversions presented unique difficulty. In other less developed lands, the State stressed the importance of rituals and iconography due to subpar literacy rates in those areas. By contrast, in the homeland, religion was for more streamlined. If one met the government's expectations, they could expect eternal paradise after their passing. Believing in *The Book of Vexrus* was not considered to be a religious practice in the traditional sense. 'Religion' implied that faith was a requirement, but the existence of an afterlife was a proven reality, one upon which all of Visryan's civil institutions were built. Citizens could track their afterlife progress online, and prisoners often requested that they be given hard labor to work off their transgressions. Churches were a relic of an uncivilized past. Why should anyone waste their time hearing a lengthy sermon when they could guarantee salvation by following the State's guidelines and working to the State's benefit?

The Book of Vexrus contained proofs of the existence of Vexrus, our god. Various unexplained phenomena compiled by the Scholars, the publicly funded authors of the sacred book, filled every page of every edition. New proofs were added every couple of years. The year that I first began working with Reggie, a man named Philip Dawson published a paper titled "Interviews of the Dead and Dying" that catalogued statements from people on their deathbeds. Everyone interviewed, roughly three hundred people, gave detailed commentary on the process of entering the afterlife. This experiment was not a novel one. The State offered grants to well-respected medical scientists and theologians to carry out these interviews constantly, and after their results were vetted by the Scholars, they were published in an updated copy of the book. Every interview strengthened Visryan's credibility and made discovering a cheap printing process more elusive by further thickening the book.

I sent an offer to the natives accompanied by a torrent of buzzwords and, unable to continue until I received a counteroffer, I put my work aside. I spent the remainder of the workday refreshing my email, hoping for a response, and staring at Reggie's chair. The thought of him, or anyone, failing to qualify for the afterlife filled me with dread. As long as I had known him, he had served the State faithfully, but in only one week he may have damned his soul to oblivion. This thought occupied my mind until a voice over the intercom signaled the end of the workday.

The Relis Department of Public Spending building stood out from the businesses just across its property line. It was maintained entirely by volunteers working to increase their afterlife credit score. Lush green grass, meticulously carved limestone statues of various government officials, and winding sidewalks wrapping around water fixtures covered the landscape. The instant I stepped through the gate at the front of the property, however, I was bombarded with a cacophony of advertisements and opportunities. Television screens promising guaranteed salvation lined store windows. One business that I passed by every day sold 'afterlife assurance plans;' a customer would meet with an afterlife credit specialist to determine what they could do to increase their score, a service often partially subsidized by the State. Across the street stood a business that marketed to the uniquely desperate. The phrase 'Come on in! You can't take it with you!' painted across the windows in massive red letters offered faint hope to the more-than-likely damned. For a fee, they seized one's assets for a negotiated amount of afterlife credit and turned them over to the State. One could quite literally buy their way into heaven.

Further down the street stood a credit transfer center. Shortly after implementing the afterlife credit system, the Supreme Council, the State's ultimate governing body, realized that, once one had the necessary amount of points to guarantee their spot in heaven, they would either stop working entirely or kill themselves to enter paradise earlier and avoid accidentally jeopardizing their status. Why would one press on and risk losing eternity? For this reason, the State instituted two laws. One allowed afterlife credit to be transferred at a dismal exchange rate, motivating the population to continue working to save their friends and family. The other levied a postmortem fee of five hundred afterlife credits for committing suicide. One thousand credits were required to enter heaven, and the average yearly credits earned was about ninety per working person, assuming that they committed no infractions. Most single people worked for one thousand five hundred credits so that they could kill themselves without going under one thousand, freeing them from any consequences.

I recognized that these institutions were necessary for the country to function and appreciated them, but working for Visryan's Public Spending Department while surrounded by businesses that subsisted off of taxpayer money frustrated me. Thankfully, they were relegated to specific regions of the city. The majority of Relis including where I lived was populated by either housing or stores that sold basic necessities such as clothing and food. The moment I passed the bullet train station, I entered a maze of State-owned, low-rent high rises. Nearly everyone, including highly valued government employees such as myself, lived in cramped apartments with a single window. The people dotting the sidewalks could have never existed in any other country. They wore the same clothes every day, ate the same food, barely earned a living wage, and could expect to work for their entire lives, but despite this, they were happy. When the snaggle-toothed man smoking on the street corner went to work in a hazardous munitions plant, he knew with absolute certainty that heaven eventually awaited him. The greasy, unwashed children digging pocket change out of a storm drain knew that this life was temporary and that their condition would ultimately improve. *The Book of Vexrus* had focused the population into a single unified force. It offered a straightforward deal to the reader: work for the State in your earthly life, and you will be rewarded in the next one. Anyone who would refuse this offer was considered to be insane and rightfully so— they often qualified for mental health assistance from the State.

With this deal in mind, I sauntered through the rusty double doors of my housing complex and rode the rickety elevator to my apartment on the fifteenth floor. The mildew expanding across the stained hallway tiles and insects pinging against flickering light fixtures were temporary. The freezing winter air that so easily penetrated the structure was temporary. The single twin bed I saw upon opening my bedroom door was temporary. These mild inconveniences became trivial when I thought about what I would inevitably receive for my service to the State. And, as polling data illustrated, the vast majority of Visryans agreed with me.

Chapter 2

Rays of sunlight beaming through the moth holes in my curtains roused me from my sleep. I panicked for a moment, fearing that I had overslept and was late for work, before remembering that it was a holiday, Visryan's only holiday: Vexrus Day. It celebrated humanity's emancipation from death and encouraged the people to give thanks to their deity, a practice that had largely disappeared as prostration did not further the goals of the State. Songs of praise for both god and Visryan would fill the streets well into the night, and the twenty-four-hour news cycle would be dominated by tributes to Visryan's soldiers overseas who fought for others' salvation.

I typically took part in the festivities, but I had decided a month earlier, shortly after Reggie's death, that I would use my day off to satisfy my curiosity about his execution. I had called Reggie's ex-girlfriend, Ashley, a few days earlier and told her that the Department of the Interior needed to seize any of Reggie's possessions that she may have had. She expressed to me her fear about contacting the authorities. I offered to pick them up myself on my day off and she, thinking that she was potentially avoiding a police raid, readily agreed. I rolled out of bed and walked to the bathroom to get ready. I usually parted my dark hair on the side and wore a gray suit accentuated with a lapel pin that designated me as a State employee. Servants of the State were expected to be cleanshaven, well groomed, and energetic seven days a week, three-hundred sixty-four days per year, every day except for Vexrus Day, but maintaining such a lively demeanor for over a decade had left me with sunken cheeks and a streak of gray hair. State employees often looked older than their actual ages, a testament to the stressful but rewarding work we did for our god. That day, however, I wanted to appear as unassuming as possible. I left my hair uncombed and my face unshaven in an attempt to meld into the crowds, and dressed in one of the navy-blue jumpsuits given to all citizens to assure that everyone has functional clothing.

I watched a pair of children pretending to be soldiers run down the hall past me as I left my apartment. They crouched before turning a corner and held their cheap, plastic toy guns against themselves to assure that no one approaching from the connecting hallway could see them. Apparently not considering me to be a threat, they spoke about their opposition.

"If he ain't here, then he's gotta be takin' the elevator to the top floor. That's what I always do when I have to be Silva," one of the children said to the other as he gestured toward the stairs. "We can head him off when the elevator reaches the top. Come on!"

They bolted past me down the hall, nearly slipping on a splotch of mold.

"'Scuse us, mister, we gotta go kill Silva," the less-engrossed boy said before disappearing around a corner.

The game that they were playing was little more than glorified tag. Any child who grew up in a Visryan household has attempted to "kill Silva" at one point or another. Over a century ago, before the masses had accepted Visryan's teachings, Edgar Silva was arguably the most powerful man in the West. He had led a secular nation that occupied nearly half of the State's current territory before Visryan's expansion. The State rarely conquered other lands using its own resources; instead, it motivated foreign citizens to overthrow them. Visryan soldiers and arms merely supplemented the citizenry's insurrections. The allure of a guaranteed afterlife prompted many would-be adversaries to turn against their homeland. When Visryan asked other nations to dissolve and relinquish their territory, they were speaking to a nation's people instead of their leaders. As copies of *The Book of Vexrus* spread among the masses, Silva saw fit to outlaw the book and criminalize its possession. This act was common among aggressed leaders. They became desperate to crush a theocratic uprising, so they forbade the public from practicing the threatening religion. This inevitably angered the populace and led to a civil war. His officials abdicated their positions and joined the furious masses. Silva fled into exile and was ultimately chased down and hanged for his crimes against the territory's new government. Visryan then instituted a theocracy and erased that nation's name from history. The historical texts I studied in school never once mentioned the nation that preceded ours by name. That mysterious era was known only as a backwards, ignorant period where the fear of death hung over the populace.

I heard a cluster of Silva killings once outside. Children ran between and hid under fold-out tables lining the street. Thankful citizens gave one another pastries and huddled together to read proofs from the sacred book. I weaved my way through a maze of women bearing fried dough, and their elated families. A man perched on a stoop strumming a worn-out guitar serenaded passersby. I stood against the wall of a housing building to make room for a girl trying to navigate the cracked sidewalk in a pair of well-used roller skates. People dressed in military attire sat in lawn chairs in the street telling stories of their heroism to circles of enamored children. This scene repeated across the housing district. People poured into the streets from every tenement for miles around. Had I been dressed in my usual work attire, I could have expected thank-yous from every person I passed.

One of my earliest childhood memories occurred on this holiday twenty-something years prior. I was five or so and had only just begun school; I did not yet understand the importance of the suit-clad State employees being showered with praise, but the attention they commanded made me think they were celebrities. One such man stood in a crowd of people who were congratulating him on receiving his fifteen-hundredth afterlife point at such a young age. He had worked as an assistant to the Scholars for over a decade, one of the most honorable, credit-rich jobs offered by the State, and one to which many people aspired. When the crowd began to scatter, my father took my hand, and we walked up to him. The man was grinning from ear to ear, nearly crying from happiness. He shook my father's hand and then knelt to shake mine.

"Listen, young man. If you dedicate your life to the State, you can be in my position one day," he said.

I just stared at him in awestruck silence. I had never seen someone so universally respected, borderline worshipped by those around him. I nodded my head, and he stood upright and spoke with my father. My mother then approached and congratulated him. He chatted with my parents for a while before being called away by another group of gushing adorers. Before departing, he looked back at me and said, "Paradise awaits!"

By the next morning, he was dead by his own hand at the age of twenty-eight. At the time, I did not understand what exactly had transpired, but as an adult, I admired and envied him. Life revolved around entrance to the afterlife. There was no greater aspiration than suicide following a career of public service. It was the ultimate reward for which all citizens strove.

After traversing miles of the hospitable labyrinth, I reached Ashley's housing complex. Aside from the different number plastered to the building's visage, hers resembled mine. Cramped hallways, leaky ceiling tiles, and shaking elevators characterized essentially every housing complex that I had ever visited, acceptable accommodations considering the taxpayer money being saved. I knocked on her door and heard her scramble to answer. I figured that she had no interest in talking to her treasonous ex-boyfriend's friends for any longer than necessary.

"So, I guess you're here for Reggie's shit?"

She blocked what little of her apartment I would have been able to see with her body and seemed to want to keep me at arm's length.

"That's the plan. You need some help getting it all together?"

"No, it's taken care of." She reached just inside and produced a sizable cardboard box. "This is everything he kept here. Did y'all already raid his place?"

If she had felt any sympathy for Reggie, she would have already been arrested. I thought she only wanted to walk away from the situation and forget about him and hopefully me, a service that I was happy to offer.

"Yeah, his place got turned over."

I took the box from her, and she started to retreat inside. Before leaving, I felt it necessary to ensure that, as far as she was concerned, the matter was closed.

"You aren't under any kind of investigation by the way. I leave with this box, and you won't ever hear from us again. Though, it is probably for the best if you don't talk about any of this."

She exhaled and smiled.

"Thanks, Marlow. I know you don't like any of this either. Happy Vexrus Day and thank you for your service."

Reggie had never told her about the nature of our work in accordance with his non-disclosure agreement, so saying that I was representing the Department of the Interior was believable. If I were to be caught, lying about working for that institution would have led to several years in prison and a considerable reduction of my afterlife score, but no other State employee was qualified to demand that she hand over potentially problematic materials. Besides, if I were to expose some sort of anti-State conspiracy, I could have reached fifteen-hundred credits in an instant.

I held the box over my head and repeated 'excuse me' ad nauseam to traverse the crowds again. Despite knowing that no agency knew or cared where I was or what I was doing, I did not try to run for fear of rousing suspicion from a hypothetical investigator. At the end of my trek, I saw a group of women huddled around the entrance to my housing complex talking with Anette, a woman from my floor. I tried to slide between them without speaking, but they recognized me despite my mediocre trappings and unshaven face.

"Marlow? Oh, sweetie why are you dressed like that? No one is gonna recognize you for your special day." Anette put her hand on my shoulder and motioned to her friends. "Everyone, this is Marlow, and he works for the government."

"Oh my! Happy Vexrus Day and thank you for your service!" one of them said and patted me on the back with her sticky, sugar coated hand.

Another held her doughnut in her mouth and mumbled some muffled pleasantries before trying to hug me.

"Thank you for the praise, ladies, but I really need to get to work. Have a good holiday." I excused myself and bolted for the elevator, relieved to hear them change the subject behind me.

Once inside my apartment, I sat down and peeled myself out of my sweat-logged jumpsuit. I put on a pair of rubber gloves I had purchased for the occasion. I thought these precautions to be appropriate, considering that tampering with and hiding evidence of this magnitude could result in a lengthy prison sentence. I would briefly see what had gotten Reggie arrested, understand why his executioners ignored procedure, and throw it away along with his memory, but what I saw before me after removing the lid struck me as anti-climactic. Aside from a few folders filled with papers, there were only three outdated copies of the *Book of Vexrus*.

I had not known what to expect, but this seemed far from treasonous.

The book cover had not substantially changed since its first printing. The golden State seal, a trio of crowns each labeled differently arranged in a triangle, stood out against a black background. I picked up what I thought to be the oldest of the three and looked it over. The letters under each crown had nearly worn off. The two that formed the bottom of the triangle were labeled "the people" and "the State," and the one at the top was labeled "Vexrus." The message below it had faded years ago, but it would have said "Through Service to Vexrus, All Become Kings." The older books were a bit thinner than the current iteration. This was to be expected as new proofs were continually added over the years. Outdated copies of the book were typically burned by the State or thrown away as they were no longer useful, but owning one, to my knowledge, had never been a crime. The government frequently held recycling drives to reuse paper from old books to print new ones, proclaiming that turning in what had become "useless relics" was morally correct. Outdated copies rarely survived these events, but if they had, they would have been given little attention. The book was sacred for about a year before it was replaced by a different, equally sacred version.

I read through the index and recognized many of the famous proofs. After all, a State employee was expected to be somewhat of an expert in the field. The manner in which the sections were separated resembled the current version. I browsed past the Simultaneous Message proofs. These were instances of multiple identical phenomena occurring before at least five witnesses per instance at roughly the same time in different locations. One particularly famous example occurred entirely outside of Visryan. Foreign peoples who had likely never been exposed to the doctrine were instructed to report a set of phrases to the government by some sort of hallucination. When critics pondered the purpose of a miracle that served only to validate itself, State researchers argued that a proven miracle strengthens belief, inspiring citizens to work harder and helping them to be at peace with death. Vexrus was thought to be a kind god, one that would prove his own existence repeatedly to reassure its people that their space in eternity was real and secure.

After this section, I came to one that I did not recognize. It was labeled "Proofs Relating to the Manalogical Sciences" and occupied nearly a fifth of the book. I had spent the better part of my childhood learning about *The Book of Vexrus*. Belief in it constituted the core around which society revolved. It was the moral compass of every citizen, official, and countless foreigners alike. I knew that there could not possibly have been a section I was unaware of. I was certain that I had never heard the term "Manalogical Sciences," nor could I define the term based on its etymology. I was clueless as to what the prefix Mana referred. I retrieved a current copy of the book from my nightstand and opened it to the

Simultaneous Proofs section in the index. The familiar Visryan Symbolism Phenomena section followed directly after it; there was no mention of manalogical science to be found. I returned to the older copy and began examining the proofs. The first was labeled "Dr. Marcus Heinz's Mana Wave Interpretation Proof." The remainder of the page was mostly covered in symbols that were entirely alien to me. The type's structure seemed to suggest that this was some sort of equation. My working theory was that these were mathematical proofs borne from a branch of science with which I was unfamiliar.

I pulled the remaining two copies out of the box and turned to their indexes. The newer one contained a section on the Manalogical Sciences, but in the older one, the section was omitted. I opened to the back covers of all three to find the year of their releases. The oldest was printed in 2253, the one I read first was dated 2254, and the newest was from 2276. The manalogical section must have appeared between the former two years. I assumed that the older books were likely forgeries. If this was the case, then Reggie being convicted of dissemination of false information made sense. Fakes such as these weakened the masses' faith and caused spikes in depression diagnoses, reduced economic output, and an increase in anti-government activity. It was for this reason that knowingly spreading false information about Vexrus or the State became a crime.

I was unable to glean any useful information from any of the remaining manalogical proofs. I briefly considered returning to Ashley's apartment to gather more information, but even if she could somehow explain these proofs, she would likely refuse to share that information with someone that she believed to represent the Department of the Interior. I then turned to the folders piled against the corner of the box. Between the two folders there could not have been more than ten pages. The hand-written portions, the majority of the pages, appeared to be Reggie's failed attempts to decipher the symbols in the manalogical sections. My best efforts to understand them were fruitless. Unsurprisingly, attempting to decode a language that may or may not have existed posed a considerable challenge. The phrase at the top of the first typed page read "My Thoughts on The Book of Vexrus and the Government that Prints It." I was thrilled to read his commentary.

"There exists evidence that The Book of Vexrus may be a work of fiction, one that I argue was created by the Visryan government. Beginning in 2254 and continuing at least through 2276, possibly longer if the pictures I have obtained are legitimate, the State added a section to the book titled Proofs Relating to the Manalogical Sciences. This section seems to revolve around a fictitious science with no basis in reality. I contacted numerous scientific and theological authorities, who I will leave

unnamed for their own protection, that could make no sense of the symbols contained within. Additionally, no historians offered any explanation beyond baseless theories. My own attempts to decipher the text over the past few months have yielded no results, and I suspect that there is no meaning to be found. At great risk to my own life and afterlife, I sought out a collector of outdated printings."

"They presented me with their own copy of the book that roused my suspicion: the 2254 printing. I poured over the manuscript and found no evidence of a Mana-logical section, but I did notice a slight difference between our copies. The leather in which his was bound was of a noticeably higher quality than mine. I initially took this to mean that mine was a forgery, but another explanation may make more sense. I hypothesize that my 2254 copy and my 2276 copies, both of which contain the section, were produced overseas to convert foreigners. Our nation, at least according to the authorities, was fairly advanced during those years and likely would have questioned an alien science, but natives on bombed-out beaches south of the equator who had never heard of Vexrus may be more inclined to believe, or so the State thought."

"The bizarre policies surrounding the book substanti-ate this theory. In addition to obtaining permission for undertaking an international flight being prohibitively difficult, copies of the book cannot leave Visryan soil. This matters little to the average citizen. After all, why bring a religious tome on vacation? Returning with copies purchased overseas, though this is an exceedingly rare occurrence, can even result in jail time even though the removal of a couple books hardly constitutes a threat to a foreign nation's religious conversion rate. The average citizen is barred from entering the poorest regions, those that are actively being colonized, entirely. I contend that the State generates different versions of the book for different groups based on what they are more inclined to believe and removes content as necessary. The necessity to maintain one's afterlife standing tends to keep citizens from questioning Visryan law, making pulling off this ruse possible. Unwavering faith in the State empowers it to inspire ever more faith in the people. Without belief in Vexrus, the State's credibility diminishes and things that would normally be considered necessary to further their noble goal of helping the masses enter eternity become sinister.

For the first time in my life, I fear both death as well as the State.

– Reginald Finster"

I set the papers down and retreated to my couch. I lay back clutching *The Book of Vexrus* and watched my wobbly ceiling fan struggle to spin. Never before had the validity of the book been questioned. Everyone I had ever met shared the knowledge that every decent citizen went to heaven. It was guaranteed, like the sun rising in the morning and setting in the evening. I held the book above my face and flipped through the pages considering the possibility that every word printed on them was false. As the possibly fake proofs that life was eternal fluttered by, a sense of unique panic manifested inside of me. I dropped the book and felt my heart begin to race. This was a type of fear unknown to the Visryan people, one that elicited dread beyond the inborn fear of death.

My first instinct was to disbelieve, but somewhere in the recesses of my mind, I began to ponder oblivion. As I dwelled on such a horrid possibility, my breathing quickened. Tears blurred my vision as I tried to comprehend the sensation of non-existence. Despite doubting the validity of Reggie's findings, the concept of my own mortality sufficed to plunge me into torment. Could the axis around which every aspect of Visryan life revolved be a work of fiction?

I could not steady myself. Reggie had reduced me to a shaking, groaning bundle of soulless cells. What a relief it would have been to shatter my window and jump to my death. Surely, an eternity of non-existence would be preferable to a life spent living in fear of it. I would have to endure for only the distance from my apartment to the pavement and not a second longer. Twenty minutes earlier, if a government official had asked me to slit my own throat and bleed to death for the State, I would have done so and thanked them for the opportunity.

Chapter 3

I know not how long I sat writhing in misery on my couch, but I did not collect myself until well after nightfall. After I regained my composure, I retrieved a pack of cigarettes and a lighter from my nightstand and returned to the couch. I rarely smoked, and certainly not indoors, but this constituted a special case. I turned on the lights and stared at my dismal apartment. It felt strange that, despite my newfound dread, the world around me continued as if nothing happened. If I listened closely, I could still hear a woman on the floor above me chattering and plodding around her kitchen. The tired shouts of children exhausted by the day's events echoed through the halls, and people cleaned spilled sugary messes off of the sidewalks outside. In a jubilant city, I alone was miserable. At least I knew that Ashley had not investigated the box's contents, perhaps only to keep her fingerprints off of the pages. If she had, she would have feared the Department of the Interior far too much to meet with a State official. Regardless of whether or not Reggie's findings were real or fake, the very notion that they had introduced reduced me to nothing—a concept yet unknown to the masses, a secret between me and a dead man.

I watched my smoke clouds dance in the gusts from the ceiling fan before dissipating into oblivion. They were transient, fleeting. They did not matter, and once I forgot about them, they would be irrevocably consumed by time. My first instinct was not to seek out support for Reggie's claims. That would only worsen my already fragile mental condition. I needed professional help. The State provided faith counseling to those who requested it, but this was typically reserved for the insane. If a government employee, especially one with ties to someone who was recently executed for disseminating false information, were to request such a service, it would have aroused suspicion. I wanted so desperately to unlearn what I had read. I would have latched on to anyone or anything that could have returned me to my ignorant state. Part of me hated Reggie. He chose me to witness his execution. He nodded at me during the obviously fake statement, knowing that it would intrigue me. He must have known that I, being a responsible State employee and loyal theocrat, would investigate the circumstances surrounding his death. He forced me into this position deliberately. The pity that I had once felt for him became a distant memory. I considered burning the box and damning his secret to oblivion along with him, but doing so would not have alleviated my suffering. If I destroyed the books without first regaining my faith, I could lose the silver bullet hidden within them that proved they were fake.

Though I had managed to calm myself, I knew that I could not live with this thought gnawing at the back of my mind for years. I would walk to work every day worrying that my life led to nothingness. Requesting counseling would not have been a viable option until years after Reggie's death when it would no longer arouse suspicion. I decided to take a day off and visit the Institute of Vexrus Studies across town hoping to find a Scholar who could answer my questions. The Institute often attracted tourists from other regions and hosted numerous school-sponsored trips throughout the year. I could blend into the crowd and speak with someone who genuinely enjoyed answering difficult questions about the book without once telling them who I was. Once I knew that the afterlife existed beyond doubt, I could return home, burn Reggie's books, and try to forget that such a bizarre theory had ever existed. For a government employee, missing work without a valid excuse could result in a reduction of one's afterlife score by up to ten points and would, if anyone saw fit to investigate Reggie's acquaintances, draw attention to me. I would claim that I had been sick on both Vexrus Day as well as the day after and did not think to obtain proof of sickness from a doctor, hoping that a lenient administrator would overlook it.

The next morning, I took a taxi to the far side of town, guaranteeing that no one with whom I was acquainted would see me. I wore another standard-issue jumpsuit and neglected to shave once again. Looking like myself would have been a liability. At a stop light, I watched two children rummage through a dumpster in an alley. The older one sorted through the trash and handed edible items to the younger one. The younger one inspected a half-eaten moldy sandwich, removed the top bun, and began eating what remained. He wiped his hands on his ill-fitting t-shirt before eating. Passersby paid them little attention. Scenes such as this were common throughout most of the nation. There was no need to help them; barring a particularly egregious act, any child who was unable to care for themselves would be sent to heaven regardless of their afterlife score. Some regions had instituted kill centers for abandoned children. This was considered to be a humanitarian accomplishment. They went to the next world and skipped a life living in squalor, and the cities remedied overcrowding in homeless shelters.

"I know, right? Wouldn't you kill to be in their shoes?" the taxi driver said, looking back at me. I knew what he meant.

"It would be pretty nice to cut the crap and be finished here. Imagine getting to heaven in eight years without even knowing what afterlife credit is."

He laughed and began driving again. I now had to question my attitude towards children such as these. Assuming that the government's afterlife policies were legitimate, these children did indeed enjoy a unique level of certainty in regard to their afterlife, but if the afterlife was a work of fiction or if the State had no control over it at all, then they would live in filth for their entire short lives for nothing. The State had no apparatus to utilize them. It simply freed them from any responsibility and left them to die. It may have appeared cruel, but their eternal reward easily outweighed any earthly suffering. Even as an elementary school student, I was taught that children like these ones were not to be pitied; instead, their existence illustrated the State's mercy.

He let me out in front of the Institute, and I paid in cash, not wanting to leave evidence that I had skipped work on a credit card bill. This building, being supported by public funds, enjoyed the same opulence as the one in which I worked. Carvings of famous statesmen offering copies of the sacred book to distraught foreigners covered the stone archway above the doors. Every shrub lining the path to the entrance had been meticulously manicured into perfectly straight edges. The inside met the same high standards. Glossy hardwood floors led into a large, open room filled with wrought iron iconography and depictions of historical battles and achievements. A statue of Department of the Interior agents bowing before the sacred book sat in the room's center. I took in a deep breath of warm air, enjoying the power of a public building's heater. The calm atmosphere and plethora of information available soothed my ailing mind.

"Sir, is there anything I can help you with?" a chipper young woman with a nametag that read 'Cindy' asked.

"Oh, yes, please. I was wondering where the Scholars are?" Cindy looked puzzled. Evidently, few people came in search of the experts.

"That's a rare request. Take the elevator to the third floor; I'm sure they'll be thrilled to have a visitor!" I thanked her and headed upstairs.

It seemed that the average citizen did not have any burning questions that they wanted answered. The third floor lacked the elegance of the entrance. It was a cramped labyrinth of hallways and closed office doors. The only signs of life were constantly ringing phones and whirring printers. I approached the secretary sitting in front of the elevator.

"Hi, I have some questions about *The Book of Vexrus* and was wondering who I should go talk to," I said. She raised an eyebrow and looked me over.

"Sure, might I ask what sort of questions?"

I swallowed and thought for a moment. I had to present myself in such a way that she did not conclude that my faith was wavering.

"Nothing all that serious. I'm wondering about an outdated edition's organization methods." I said, trying to maintain a conversational tone.

She seemed to lose all interest in me and my dull questions.

"You're looking for Albert Woodward. He's in office 315 just down the hall, fifth door on your right." She leaned over her desk and pointed me in the right direction before turning her attention to a phone call.

Scratches in the hallway's dark blue paint guided me towards my destination. The finish peeled from the floor and there was visible water damage on the ceiling. The windows on every office door in the hallway were covered with paper. Any voices that may have been behind the doors were drowned out by a whirring air conditioning unit at the end of the hallway. I reached Woodward's door and knocked, causing the loose lock to rattle. I heard no sound and feared that he may have left early. I peered through a gap between the sagging door and the doorframe but could see no movement. I struck the side of door more forcefully. I did not want to make my desperation known, but I would not be ignored.

"Hello? Is anyone in there?" The secretary leaned into the hallway to investigate, but the door swung open before she could confront me.

"God damn, can you give me a minute to answer?" a hunched-over old man said, looking up at me through thick spectacles.

"Sorry. I'm just a bit pressed for time. Can I ask you a couple of questions?"

I watched the secretary retreat out of the corner of my eye.

"I guess so. That's one of the things they pay me to do after all." he said and hobbled back into his office, cane in hand, motioning me to follow. "Close the door behind you. I hate the racket from that damn machine!"

I obeyed, relieved to be free of any potential hazardous witnesses. This was not the warm welcome that the friendly woman at the entrance promised me. It was strange to see someone of such advanced age. The Scholars, despite their cosmically important, credit-rich positions, almost never opted for suicide. They refused to do so out of a sense of duty to their fellow man. This willingness to risk eternity to serve the people earned them considerable respect. My parents ascended to heaven in their mid-forties, as did most people. As a child, I viewed them as something of a novelty. The adults around me would tell me to be grateful for their sacrifice. They suffered through earthly life for twice as long as those around them in the pursuit of helping as many people as possible ascend with them.

I expected to see books, specifically copies of *The Book of Vexrus* and books relating to it, piled to the ceiling, but aside from him, a desk, two chairs, and a computer, the office was nearly empty. It was a cheap little box made of chipped drywall and broken ceiling tiles. I was surprised that a public institution, especially one with such an immaculate façade, would leave its offices in such a decrepit state. He pointed me to a chair in the middle of the cramped room while he reclined in another behind his desk. He groaned and leaned forward onto the desk, folding his hands in front of him.

"So, what is it you wanted to ask me?" he said and smiled, cocking his head to one side, leaving no trace of his former aggressive persona.

"A while back, a friend, well more of an acquaintance, showed me some old copies of *The Book of Vexrus* that had some inconsistencies that I hoped you could explain." I said.

"Who keeps old copies of the book?" he said, squinting and scratching his chin.

"Just some dumbass that used to live in my building. Haven't seen him in five or six years. I hadn't thought about it until it came up in conversation with a friend recently."

I gritted my teeth, hoping that he would not view me as a threat to the State.

"Well, do you have any of these old copies?"

"No. He wouldn't even let me hold them."

"That's too bad, I'd love to see them. If you ever get ahold of them, you ought to bring them by here. I bet the boys downstairs would get a kick out of them. What kind of inconsistencies were in them? I'm sure I've probably seen them before. The same fakes tend to resurface every so often."

"There were a few different copies. Some of them contained a section labeled Proofs Relating to the Manalogical Sciences, and some didn't. The proof I looked at was incomprehensible. It was just a sequence of symbols that I had never seen before."

He took his hands off of the desk and reclined with a giggle.

"A classic fake! I get one of these things every year without fail. Those copies come from somewhere overseas. I can't quite recall the details, but some foreigner tried to make fakes with ridiculous sections to turn citizens against the State. Don't you worry."

He understood the fear that these fraudulent books inspired; he must have dealt with distraught citizens from time to time.

"So, the government never printed any books like that? He just had a bunch of fakes?" I said in a hopeful tone.

"Nope. Never."

I breathed a sigh of relief. My faith had been restored. This confident old man had spent the entirety of his life studying the book and explaining its perceived inconsistencies. My concerns were trivial for a man of his status. I was but another in a long line of misled citizens that he had pulled from the brink of oblivion. The State returned to its exalted status and the afterlife shifted back into place.

"Do you think you could give me that guy's name?" he asked as he retrieved a notebook and a pen from his desk drawer. "Now don't worry, I don't want to put him in jail. I just can't let him mislead good people like you. You understand, right?"

I stuttered for a moment, searching my mind for a scapegoat, real or imagined.

"Honestly, I don't think he ever even gave me his full name. He just bombarded me with conspiracy theories on occasion, and that was about the extent of our relationship. I'd help you if I could."

I stood and started to leave. I should have known that any State employee I spoke with would want to investigate, but I was too desperate to care.

"Well, what did you call him?" he said and clicked his pen a few times. I looked off to the corner of the room, pretending to be lost in thought.

"I think it was James or maybe John. I wish I could remember more." His brow wrinkled and he let out a sharp exhale.

"Do you remember what he looked like? Tattoos? Deformities?"

"He was white. Late twenties to early thirties. No deformities, and I'm not sure about any tattoos. He always wore one of these jumpsuits." I said and started for the door again.

He looked down at his blank paper and spoke again as I turned the doorknob.

"Can I get your name?"

I felt the urge to bolt out of his office. I knew that he would at least run a background check on any name I gave him, and giving a false name could warrant an investigation. I looked at him over my shoulder. He could denounce me as a heretic, and the circumstances surrounding me might prove him to be correct in the eyes of the law.

"Edward Delaney. Now, I really must be going. Thank you for your time, and if I get ahold of any of those books, I'll bring them to you." I said and left without turning around to face him.

As the door closed behind me, I heard his pen scribbling across the paper. I hoped that the fake name I had given him would delay any coming investigation. Perhaps, I had portrayed myself as sufficiently non-threatening, and he would deem a background check unnecessary.

I hailed a cab and paid extra for him to speed. I told him to drop me off four buildings down from my own and waited until he drove away to sprint back to my apartment. I do not know if anyone recognized me, but I had striven for complete anonymity. Seeing that others were on the elevator, I elected to use the stairs. Running up fifteen flights left me sweaty and out of breath. I looked down the hallway in both directions and was relieved to see that no one saw me. I hurried to my apartment, went inside, and locked the door behind me. Nothing seemed to have been tampered with. There were no shoeprints on the carpet, nor were any of my possessions moved. My faith was saved but my soul may not have been. I had expected him to ask from where my questions about the book originated, but his insistence worried me. If I was not under some type of investigation before speaking with him, I was after.

I knelt down and reached under the couch. I felt around until I found Reggie's books and pulled them out one by one. If any government agent were to find these books, I would be arrested. I took them to the bathroom and sat on the tile. I did not want to leave my apartment until they had been destroyed. I opened the first one to its managlogical section and began tearing out pages. I tore each page into smaller pieces and, once I had torn up four pages, flushed them. I repeated the process until the section was gone. I wanted to throw away each one of the books in this manner but knew that using such a large amount of water could result in my landlord investigating the cause. And if I clogged a pipe somewhere in the building with evidence of a capital crime, I would be both arrested as well as made into a laughingstock. Keeping the books was far too risky, though. Even if a State official did not discover them, a random citizen could, and I could not in good conscience allow such terrible objects to fall into someone else's hands. I needed to get them out of my possession as quickly as possible. Even if the Department of the Interior suspected that I had experienced a crisis of faith, a lack of hard evidence coupled with my employment status and record may ward them off.

I briefly considered skipping work until I had gradually disposed of the books through the building's plumbing system. There was a public bathroom on every floor; I could flush a number of pages per floor over the course of a week or so and be rid of all but their leather bindings, but I had already skipped one day of work and shown myself in public. Missing work would inevitably be interpreted as a sign of guilt in an ensuing investigation. A faithful, healthy citizen always arrived at their job on time and was grateful for the opportunity to serve the State. Burning them as soon as possible was the logical choice. There was no incinerator in my building, however, nor was there one within walking distance. Carting evidence of treason around town looking for a spot to burn it would not have been tactical, and starting a trashcan fire in front of my home in broad daylight would also have been fairly conspicuous. I then recalled that an incinerator must have sat in in the basement of my office building. Shortly after the signal ending the workday blared though every office, the janitorial staff carried the day's garbage to an elevator. Not once had I ever seen a garbage truck leave the property, and the State tried to avoid such unsightly things near important public buildings.

Before bringing the books to work, I needed to ensure that there was indeed an incinerator. I might be asked why I skipped work as well and having them on my person during such questioning could be disastrous. I decided to hide them for the next day and destroy them the day after, once I knew that I was not under any suspicion. I stacked the books on top of one another in the bottom of a garbage bag followed by Reggie's manuscript and other work, tied the bag off, and wrapped it in plastic. I then removed the lid from the tank behind my toilet and lowered it inside. I forced it down with the handle of a broom until the lid could be replaced, covered it, and prayed to a god that I was happy to believe in again that no one would find it. Vexrus was a merciful god. He knew that I had been led astray and would never threaten the State or His supremacy. I just hoped that I could convince the State that that was true.

Chapter 4

I woke up early the next morning and cleaned myself up. I shaved and spent the better part of an hour molding the hair that I had taken such care to leave messy back into its rigid, parted on the right, Department of Public Spending-recommended form. I buried the jumpsuit that I had worn for the past two days at the bottom of my dirty clothes hamper and donned my usual suit and tie. I inspected both my hiding spot as well as the area where I had examined Reggie's items. Aside from a few scraps of paper resting behind the toilet and the unassuming box that had contained them, there was no visible trace of any evidence. I stuffed the scraps into my pocket and took the box with me when I left. I tossed the box into the garbage can in front of my building and stopped to survey my surroundings. People trotting to work lined the streets. I heard the faint chirping of birds perched on windowsills far above me, occasionally drowned out by a passing car. Nothing deviated from the norm.

On my walk to work, once I was certain that I was alone, I sprinkled the scraps into a storm drain. Had they known the details of my predicament, the people walking past me on the sidewalk would have thought I was being needlessly paranoid, but they did not know nearly as much as I about the inner workings of the Department of the Interior. If you posed the question, 'What do your taxes pay for?' to the average citizen, they would have probably guessed that the majority of spending goes to healthcare and housing, but the Department of the Interior enjoys just as much funding as either of these, and their budget grows every year. I knew that the work they did behind the scenes was crucial to the State's survival. Of course, I also feared what such a militarized force could do to me, especially when given carte blanche.

Had I been guilty of any other crime, I would not have been nearly as concerned, but to damage the people's faith, or to possess materials that could have done so, was one of the highest crimes in the State. It was an attack on the principles upon which Visryan was founded and was shockingly easy to be accused of. By simply possessing Reggie's banned materials, I could be charged with conspiring to damage the people's faith. In an instant, the State could deploy a legion of spies and interrogators to hunt down the guilty and obtain proof of their crimes. I would have given anything to have never opened that box. I rushed the rest of the way. Every car that appeared to slow down as it passed frightened me. There was no way to know whether or not I was being investigated. It was entirely possible that Albert had neglected to investigate such a non-threatening figure as my-self. He also may have been unable to identify me or may have assumed that he had misheard me when running a background check on the name I had given him.

Upon reaching the building, I hurried inside, keeping my eyes forward until I reached the elevator. I wanted to re-as-similate into the publicly funded machine and disappear. Once inside, I fixed my eyes on the keypad and pressed floor three, my floor, without looking up. I was a faceless suit on his way to work, uninterested in paying attention to whoever may have been meandering around the ground floor.

When I exited the elevator, the administrator in charge of my floor, a middle-aged man named Oswald, approached me. He was tall and thin with a rigid face completely devoid of emotion. The loose skin on his cheeks hung below his glasses and shifted slightly with each step. Despite his stern appearance, I had always liked him. For a bureaucrat, he had an impressive amount of empathy for those beneath him.

"Marlow, why were you absent yesterday? And why didn't you call in and tell us you weren't going to show up?" he said.

He sounded genuinely concerned.

"Oh, I'm sorry I must've forgotten to call. I've been sick for the last two days, but I'm feeling much better now. Do I need to get tested?"

Oswald shook his head.

"No, it's alright. Just remember to call next time, okay?"

"I will. Sorry for the inconvenience."

Oswald wandered around the room and spoke with the other employees. I let out a sigh of relief. Had I been required to prove that I had actually been sick, I may have been in trouble, but employees with a record as exemplary as mine were usually given a degree of leniency, especially when working for someone as lax as him.

I left my office door open so that I could observe the janitorial staff when they passed by. I checked my email and was excited to see that I had finally gotten a response from one of the foreign leather merchants. He agreed to sell the State one-thousand hides for sixteen hundred dollars each, a fairly equitable deal. This would provide enough leather for copies of the book to be distributed across a dozen colonies. I responded with a string of pleasantries and thanked him for his cooperation. Of course, I included a few lines of flowery rhetoric thanking him for furthering the goals of the divine. When discussing Vexrus in any capacity related to our work, we were encouraged to use grandiose language that conveyed just how cosmically significant our work was. My most frequently cited authority aside from the sacred book was "Vexrus' will." In addition to financial compensation, those who produced products for the State enjoyed a handsome amount of afterlife credit if they gave Visryan a discount. This leverage made negotiating contracts a simple task.

While I was typing a summary of the deal for the higher-ups, a janitor pushed a cart past the doorway to my office. Mountains of discarded files and coffee-stained papers nearly obscured his vision. He waved to me and continued forward, whistling a shapeless tune. I left my desk and tailed him, keeping about ten feet behind. He turned a corner in front of me towards the service elevator. I hurried to the breakroom near the elevator and watched him. He pressed the down arrow on the keypad and pushed the cart inside. The LED screen above the elevator doors ticked down to floor B2. The incinerator must have been in the subbasement. I poured myself a cup of coffee and sat down in a dented folding chair in the corner of the room. The clock on the wall beside me said 12:43 p.m. Employee breaks were not to exceed twenty minutes, but if a higher-level employee were to scold me, my earlier accomplishment would hopefully grant me leniency.

I sat undisturbed for five minutes or so before a man from the opposite side of my floor walked into the room. One hand tugged on his immaculate bowtie while his other wrestled a Styrofoam cup from a plastic sleeve.

"Hey there, Marlow. How are you getting by without Reginald?" he said.

I looked up at him for a moment before responding, studying him. A strand of over-gelled hair hung down in the center of his forehead.

"I'm fine, Jim. He was a good employee and all, but I don't want to work with anyone like him," I said, shrugging as I sipped my coffee.

"It was false information, right? That's what they got him for?" He pulled up a chair beside me and leaned towards me, his eyes fixated on my face.

"Yeah, that's it."

I craned my head upwards and drank the rest of my coffee, giving me a break from his stare.

"What kind of information was it anyway?" He said, cocking his head.

I froze.

"How the hell should I know?"

I stood to throw away my cup.

"You guys were friends, weren't you?" he said and followed me.

"I liked the guy and all, but we weren't that close."

I began to fear that he was asked to question me. I was not well acquainted with this man; aside from passing glances and an occasional wave, we had rarely spoken to one another. Were it not for office meet and greets, I would not have known his name. The Department of the Interior often recruited civilians to assist them with investigations, enticing them with afterlife credit.

"Come on, I'm just curious," he kept prodding.

"If I knew anything, I would tell you, but I don't," I answered.

I tossed my cup in the garbage and stepped away from him. He exhaled and departed from the breakroom without a word. This bizarre exchange renewed my paranoia. I feared that the State may have considered me to be a threat after all.

I meandered around the room for a few more minutes before I heard the elevator doors open again. The same janitor that I had followed earlier walked out pushing a cart with a now empty trashcan on it. This confirmed my theory. I looked up at the clock and saw that it was now 1:15 p.m. Assuming that he did not stop to speak with anyone or face any unexpected difficulty, It took him thirty-two minutes to reach the incinerator, dump the garbage and return to this floor. He pushed his cart down the hall in the direction opposite my office and turned a corner. I hurried back to my office, hoping that no managers had noticed the length of my break. I repeated "B2 thirty-two minutes" until I was confident that I had memorized it.

I did not speak to a single person for the remainder of the day. I sent the summary of my dealings with the leather merchant to the administrators and almost immediately received a congratulatory email. I asked if they had anything else for me to work on, but they never responded. Being without work was a rare occurrence but not unheard-of. Every couple of months or so, Reggie and I would find ourselves at work with nothing to do. I spent the remainder of the day worrying about what the hypothetical investigator assigned to me was doing while I was trapped at work. They could be sitting on my couch waiting to shoot me when I walked through the door. I could not allow my anxiety to show itself. There could have been an agent watching me through my webcam, searching for any twitch or utterance that could incriminate me. Perhaps that was why I was given no work to do. They wanted me alone with my thoughts, without distraction. I wandered around the office, forced down vending-machine pretzels, played sudoku on my work computer, anything to create the veneer of normalcy.

When the end-of-day announcement finally liberated me, I left without a word. I wanted to be in my apartment guarding the evidence until the next day when I could destroy it. I fantasized about returning to a life where the State was something to be worshiped instead of feared. I could soon resume being a cog in a divine machine that promised me eternity. I could follow orders and reap my reward.

As I left the property, I saw a black car with nearly opaque windows resting outside of the gate. I half-expected the doors to fly open and produce agents from the Department of the Interior, but it just sat there. There were people inside, and I could hear the engine running. It must have been a State-owned car; it was illegal for a citizen to tint their windows so darkly, and if one did, they would not park next to constantly surveilled public property. After I passed it, its headlights turned on and illuminated the street in front of me. Its engine revved and it squeaked out onto the street. I stood and clinched my fists. This was the end, I thought. I was about to be arrested. The car approached and barreled past me down the street in a column of wind. Though it had passed me by, this event sufficed to strengthen my paranoia once again. I sprinted down the sidewalk, worried that the car was headed to my apartment. It was heading in the direction of my building, after all.

When I reached my housing complex, I rushed upstairs to my apartment without acknowledging any of the people scattered about the entrance. The suspicious nature of my behavior did not cross my mind; I would not feel secure until I knew that the evidence was still hidden. I opened the door and was relieved to see that the apartment was unmolested. I saw no evidence of tampering with any of my possessions. No couch pillows had been moved, no unfamiliar stains on the carpet, every door and cabinet that was closed when I left was still closed now, and no lights had been turned on. I tossed my tie and jacket onto the couch, walked into the bathroom, and removed the lid from the toilet tank. The plastic-wrapped garbage bag sat in the bottom of the tank where I had left it. Relief washed over me. I exhaled and rubbed my tired eyes. I pulled it out and set it down in the bathtub to dry before opening it.

I sometimes brought my lunch to work and thought that I could break the books down into smaller pieces, hide them in a brown paper bag, and leave them in the office refrigerator until I could dispose of them. I could write "out of order" on a piece of paper and tape it to the restroom on my floor shortly before taking a break to eat. I planned on eating early, at ten-forty-five, assuring that I would be alone in the breakroom. Once I was certain that no one was looking in my direction, I could slip onto the elevator and hunt for the incinerator. If I were to be asked why I were down there, I could argue that I was searching for a working bathroom.

"Well, why did you come to this floor to find one?" a janitor might have asked.

"The restroom on my floor is out-of-order." I would respond.

He would point me in the direction of a restroom and leave me unbothered. Once someone realized that the third-floor bathroom worked, the evidence would have already been destroyed. In the worst-case scenario, I would be scolded for pulling a childish office prank, and, while that may hurt my reputation, it would be preferable to imprisonment or execution.

I retrieved a brown paper bag and a pair of scissors and sat down on the bathroom floor. I cut into the plastic and pulled out the garbage bag. The sides of the bag were more stretched out than I recalled and the pile in the bottom of it looked lop-sided. I tore the bag open and saw that the stack of books had fallen to one side. I shrugged and began pulling them out, thinking little of it until I saw Reggie's manuscript sandwiched between two of the books. I remembered placing it on top of them. I knew that I had. I set the paper down and searched around the base of the toilet. I saw no foot-prints or scraps of paper. Nothing suggested that anyone had been in my bathroom, but somehow, the paper had been moved. I elected to pour myself a drink to calm my nerves before continuing. As I walked out of the bathroom, I saw a long black hair peeking out of the shadow underneath the door. I held it up to the light. It could not have belonged to any guest that I had entertained in recent memory, and it certainly did not belong to me. I cleaned frequently; this could not have been a relic of a long-gone visitor. Someone knew my secret.

Chapter 5

I was hopeless. Once they realized that I could not lead them to other heretics, they would manifest from some shadowy corridor to carry out my punishment. Eventually, on my way to work or perhaps in my sleep, the Department of the Interior would either abduct me or shoot me in the back of the head. It was entirely possible that they were monitoring me in my own apartment. I had helped to streamline the production of the millimeter-wide cameras that likely recorded me. Pulling the evidence out of its hiding place would be enough to convict me. At any moment, heavy footsteps could echo down the hall. The fist of the State would kick in my door and splatter me across the wall. I left the evidence piled on my bathroom floor. There was no reason to return it to its hiding place; they knew that I had it. I walked into the kitchen and pulled a bottle of Vodka out of the freezer. I refused to be sober when they sent me to the endless nothingness.

I plopped down on the couch, drank, and watched the door. There would be no trial for this "heretic." The public would never know what I had done and thus a public trial would be an unnecessary expenditure. Every budgeting policy for which I had fought, the policies that had given me an afterlife score of over one thousand by age thirty, would work against me. I wanted to blame Reggie, but he had simply wanted to relay what he believed to be the truth. My inability to reason clearly and my insufficient devotion to the State had reduced me to this. After ten or so painful gulps, I lost track of time. Those agents would witness exactly what exposure to banned material does to someone. I would be delirious or unconscious with vomit and drool stains on my dress shirt eager for a bullet to scramble my brain. I paid taxes for years for the State to one day free me from my mortal coil, and that was what they were going to do. Sometime after midnight, I rolled onto the floor and blacked out.

I woke up with a pounding headache laying in a puddle of liquor. It was nearly noon, and no one had come. I peeled myself off of the carpet and staggered to the bathroom. The man I saw staring at me in the mirror was not the man I had once been. He was pale with bloodshot eyes. I could have rushed to work in a futile attempt to salvage my reputation, but I could not find the energy nor motivation to do so. I was alive only in the biological sense of the word, my now-mortal soul existing on borrowed time. Under the sink I saw my cellphone. It must have fallen out when I looked through the evidence. I picked it up and held down the power button. As expected, it would not turn off. The Department of the Interior could use this feature to monitor any suspected heretic at any time. I shouted a brief string of invectives at it and hurled it into the wall over the bathtub, shattering it.

I walked into the kitchen and tore the landline phone from the wall followed by my computer. Every piece of technology I owned was a tool of those who hunted me. The television, my smartwatch, and every clock in my house had been incriminating me for days. One after another, I slammed them against the bathroom wall. The catharsis soothed my hangover. A crack spread across the wall leading down to the pile of mutilated electronics below. I turned the water on to guarantee that they were unsalvageable. A couple of sparks flashed under the current, then nothing. They had enough evidence to justify my execution twice over, but I hoped that this gesture would at least infuriate whoever was watching on the other side enough for them to storm into my apartment and question me face to face.

"You never gave a damn about me did you, Vexrus?" I said, staring at myself in the mirror. "What kind of a god punishes a man that served Him for thirty-five and a half years? I looked in that box instead of carrying it straight to a police station, and for that crime, you're cutting me off from heaven?"

I tore the mirror from the wall, not wanting to stare at the corpse I had become any longer, and tossed it on top of the pile.

"Either you're not a merciful god, or the government doesn't work for you."

I gasped and covered my mouth. Saying such a blasphemy, if heard by someone in a position of authority, constituted a crime. My anger had caused me to speak out of turn. I mumbled an apology to Vexrus and the State at roughly the same volume hoping that any remaining microphone would hear all or none of it.

I tossed my vomit-crusted shirt aside and changed into a standard-issue jumpsuit. I then washed my face in the sink and brushed my teeth. I left the books on the bathroom floor covered in the shards of a dozen shattered screens, retired to my bedroom, and pulled back the curtains on my window. I wanted to watch as the machine encircled me. Men in black uniforms huddled together in the alley beside my building. I was too high up to tell whether or not they were looking up at me, but if they were, I suspected that they could see me quite clearly. I scanned the windows of the building next to mine looking for agents but found none. They could have worn street clothes or ostentatious uniforms with gold embellishments buttoned to the collar and shiny black boots. They were the most overfunded force within Visryan's borders and operated with surgical precision. There could have been one watching me through the scope of his rifle waiting for permission to kill me. Another could have been watching me through the wall with a powerful infrared camera. A crew of them piled into a van could have been watching my every movement through a hundred tiny lenses.

Part of me knew that, if anyone else had been in my situation, I would have been cheering on the Department of the Interior like a good citizen. I had helped to fund the Department of the Interior's Relis headquarters, after all. Without heaven, I became selfish. Self-preservation had never in my life been a priority. Accidental death, assuming that one's death was indeed an accident, and death in service to the State, typically merited ascension to heaven. I had spent nearly every waking hour hoping that my death was near, but now that it finally seemed to be the case, I was afraid. I had given myself cause to be afraid. Any creak squeaking through the walls around me could have been an approaching agent. The groan of the air vent elicited a panicked response. Would they crash through the windows and fill me with lead? Would they drop down through the vent in the ceiling and slit my throat? Surely, they were at least watching me through the window. I eased the curtains back into place and backed away.

I then heard a knock at the door. There had been no heavy footsteps marching down the hall outside. The mechanical clacks I had come to associate with firearms were nowhere to be found. The knocking grew louder and more persistent. I crept to the kitchen and retrieved a knife before approaching the door. I stared through the peephole to see a surprisingly non-threatening figure. It was a rather young, short woman wearing a pristine officer uniform from the Department of the Interior; she must have had enough information to bury me. From what I could tell, she was alone. I swallowed and unlatched the door opting to fend off a single attacker rather than the reinforcements she might have brought if I had refused her entry. I held the knife at my side and cracked the door.

"You may as well let me in. I have a lot more leverage than you do right now, friend."

She made no attempt to force her way in, nor did she reach for her sidearm.

"Don't you think we would've just shot you earlier today? You were alone several times, but we chose not to. Three of my guys requested permission to shoot you a minute ago while you were looking out the window. You're not marked for dead yet."

She was right. I had no chips with which to bargain. If they wanted to storm in here and kill me, they could. I opened the door and stepped aside, gesturing towards the couch.

"Wow, you look like shit. I guess that's what banned books do to people, huh."

She narrowed her eyes at the knife at my side. Her fingers traced the holster hanging from her belt. I took this as a warning and tossed the knife to the opposite side of the room.

"Come on in, I guess."

She strode across the room and plopped down in the center of the couch. I looked back at the open door. I was confident that I could make it outside before she caught me but knew that a horde of agents would kill me once I did.

"We tried calling but…" She looked at the phone cable hanging out of the wall. "We ran into technical difficulties. Anyway, my name is Eleanor Riley and, as you can probably guess, I work for the Department of the Interior." she said in the self-satisfied tone characteristic of those in the armed services.

"So, what are you gonna do? I work for the Department of Public Spending; I know how this usually goes."

I pointed at my temple.

"If you're going to shoot me, shoot me."

I closed the door, leaned against the wall, and slid to the floor. She rolled her eyes and grunted.

"You're a depressing one, aren't you? I'm not going to do anything, at least not yet, so cheer up a little. Your afterlife isn't gone just yet."

I looked up at her, mouth agape, as if I had seen an angel.

"You really mean that?" I felt tears welling in my eyes.

"If you answer all of my questions, I do. It's not like you challenged god or took a shot at a State employee. You're far from irredeemable."

She averted her gaze, perhaps put off by my sudden emotional display. I wiped my eyes and collected myself.

"Of course, anything. What do you want to know?"

She twirled her finger through her long black hair and scanned my ruined apartment.

"How did you know that we'd been here? I would rather avoid doing house calls in the future."

"Well, I stacked the books on top of one another followed by the paper, but when I looked inside the bag, the paper was between two of the books."

"That's incompetence on my team's part."

She exhaled sharply through her nose. I hesitated to continue but wanted to answer question to the fullest extent.

"I also found a long black hair that couldn't have belonged to anyone I knew."

"Like this?"

She held out a fistful of her own hair.

"Exactly."

"Well, it's partially my fault then. I'm glad I came up here personally so I can keep that off the record. Now, could you please explain how this all came about in your own words?" Her voice took on a more serious tone as she pulled a smartphone out of her breast pocket.

"I assume you know about Reggie?"

"Reginald Finster, yes."

"Right. I was asked to witness his execution, which I did. Before the execution, the officer in charge read an obviously false statement. This was a violation of Reginald's rights and, I felt, merited an investigation. I took the box of books from his girlfriend's house without her knowledge. I don't even think she knew what was in it. Reading through them made me miserable in a way previously unknown to me. I needed reassurance but didn't want to request help from the State for fear of ruining my reputation. That's why I went to the Institute of Vexrus Studies across town and spoke with one of the Scholars, which is how I assumed you guys found out about me."

She nodded and moved her finger in a circle prompting me to continue.

"Once my faith had been restored, I planned on destroying the books and moving on with my life."

She smiled and nodded her head. She seemed to be fairly understanding.

"That's what we thought too. I'll take the books with me and burn them. Then I'll recommend that you serve, let's say, three months in a labor camp with no reduction in afterlife score. Please don't go around doing solo investigations in the future. I highly doubt that any statement delivered at an execution conducted by the Department of the Interior was false, but if it was, I assure you it was a necessary measure."

She smiled and helped me up. I was in a state of disbelief. I was going to be given a laughably lenient sentence and set free with no lasting consequences. I was saved.

"You can really do that?"

"Well, the higher ups will ultimately decide what happens to you, but I, as the captain of the team in charge of your case, have a lot of say in your punishment."

She pointed to a trio of gold stripes stitched to her breast that I assumed designated her as a captain. Her braggadocious nature may have irritated me if she had not offered me a way out.

"I'll get the books."

I fetched a bag from the kitchen, rushed to pile everything inside, and returned to the living room. I did not want her to see the mound of ruined electronics in my bathtub lest she recommend a stay in a mental hospital. She took the bag and threw it over her shoulder.

"Expect for your sentence begin in seven days or so; we prefer to allow cooperative suspects the time to make whatever preparations they need to. We'll arrange transport."

She thrust a card with her information on it into my hand.

"When you get a working phone again, call me so I have your number. That way, I can give you a heads up. After we interview Mr. Finster's former girlfriend, you'll receive your sentence. What was her name? Ashley Davidson or something like that, right?"

"Davis," I said, and held the door open for her.

"Thanks, see you soon."

She walked down the hall and disappeared onto the elevator.

I spent the remainder of the day cleaning up the mess I had made. Only hours earlier, I had resigned myself to dying in a hopeless melee against the State. The nightly news would have told the tale of the man with a kitchen knife who rushed armed agents from the Department of the Interior and died in a barrage of machine gun fire. Had another officer been in charge of my case, that may have come to pass. I still had to serve my sentence, though, and I dreaded explaining myself to Oswald. I had learned a new appreciation for the State and its mercy. I apologized to Vexrus for doubting Him. He and the State epitomized goodness and worked to the benefit of mankind. After hauling the last pile of broken electronics to the garbage, I lay back on my bed to rest, and watched the ceiling fan spin. I wondered what my sentence might entail. I may have been required to take reeducation courses while interned. I wondered if Ashley would join me. After all, she had as much involvement with Reggie as I did, and Eleanor said that she planned on interrogating her as well.

I jolted upright and clenched my jaw. When she spoke with Ashley, she would find out that I had impersonated an agent from the Department of the Interior and that I had neglected to tell her. This would allow Ashley to blame me for her not turning over the evidence. She was in a position to exonerate herself by exposing my other crimes. She could walk free by damning me to oblivion! I needed to prevent her from incriminating me. If I explained myself, I thought, she would be understanding and leave out key details during her interrogation. No one would ever have to know. I instinctively reached for my cell phone's usual location on the corner of my nightstand, but remembered that I had destroyed it to prevent the State's surveillance. I took my wallet and rushed outside to find a payphone.

It was late afternoon, and people returning home from work crowded the streets. I tore down the sidewalk sliding between pedestrians. I ran nearly two miles before finding one; after all, payphones only ever served those too poor to afford a cell phone. Two of them sat outside of one of those afterlife transfer places. An old woman stood at one haggling with some government employee over two afterlife points. Such desperation would have been unbecoming of a State employee such as myself. Eleanor had not said when she planned on speaking with Ashley. She had left my apartment a couple of hours earlier; if she went from there to Ashley's, it would already have been too late. I pushed that thought out of my mind and focused on the task at hand.

Thanks to Reggie, I knew Ashley's number. I dropped a coin into the payphone and huddled over the machine. Being heard by an eavesdropper could complicate my situation. With each passing ring, I felt the happy life I had lived days ago receding further and further into the past.

"Hello?" On the fifth ring, she answered. "Who is this?"

"Marlow. It's Marlow."

"What's up? Why would you call me?"

"Where are you now? I need to see you."

She went silent for a moment. I knew how this sounded. We were not friends and had never spent any time together aside from when I saw her with Reggie, but I could not risk asking her to lie to the Department of the Interior over an unsecure phone call.

"I'm not sure about that Marlow. You sound upset; is something wrong?"

"I'm terribly upset and need to explain why face to face. You can pick the place. Please, trust me. It is extremely important for both of us that we speak in person immediately."

I squeezed my eyes shut and clinched my fist.

"Okay. How about Eddie's? It's the diner across the street from my house. I can be there in twenty minutes."

I threw my head back and let out a sigh.

"That would be great. I'll head that way now. See you soon." I said and sprinted down the street.

Chapter 6

I saw her sitting alone through the window facing the street. I stopped running and tried to appear calm as I entered. She looked anxious, but waved to me and smiled as I opened the door. The other patrons scattered around the restaurant paid me no mind, and thankfully none of them looked like State employees. A hostess tried to seat me, but I brushed past her and approached Ashley's table.

"Hey, can we move to a table near the back?" I whispered while searching the restaurant for suspicious onlookers.

"Sure, I guess."

She took her drink and followed me to the back corner. I asked a confused waitress for coffee and waited for her to disappear into the kitchen before speaking.

"Have you been contacted by the Department of the Interior?" I asked.

"No. Isn't that your job?" She seemed more at ease and took a sip from her cup.

"Thank god," I said.

I went silent and rifled through a box of sugar packets under the window as the waitress returned.

"Should I have been? I thought you said that I could forget about Reggie now."

I narrowed my eyes at her in an attempt to make her shut up until we were alone and continued to feign interest in their selection of artificial sweeteners. The aloof waitress topped off Ashley's cup and ventured across the restaurant.

"I don't work for the Department of the Interior."

She looked uneasy and began to inch to the side of the booth to exit.

"Listen, when I went to Reggie's execution, the guards there lied about his final statement, meaning that the State didn't respect one of his rights. Do you understand?"

"That's not right. Everyone gets to do a final statement, don't they? Why couldn't he?"

"That was my thought, exactly. That's why I wanted to see what he had been up to. As I'm sure you know, he was a heretic," I explained. "The things you gave me were fake copies of *The Book of Vexrus* intended to weaken citizen faith."

"That makes sense. I didn't know what the stuff in the box was, but I thought that if I were caught with it, I would be charged with some kind of crime. Thanks for the info, but why exactly couldn't we do this over the phone?"

"The Department of the Interior is investigating the incident, and they are probably listening in on your calls."

She gasped and her eyes darted around the room.

"Am I in trouble? You said it would be fine!" She scowled.

"It will be. Quiet down. I've already talked to an officer about the incident and covered both of our tracks. I just need you to stick to the story." I lowered my voice. "We are going to be just fine."

"What story?"

"You committed a crime by knowingly keeping evidence of heresy; I committed a crime by posing as an agent for the Department of the Interior. I told Eleanor Riley, the officer in charge of this case, that I stole the box without your knowledge and said that I didn't think that you knew what it was." Ashley's hand trembled as she lifted her cup. "All you have to do is tell her that I came over to drop something off – it could be something that Reggie borrowed and left at the office. I went to the bathroom and must have stolen the box then. I found it in the back corner of your closet in my search for information about Reggie. You never knew it was there. You were looking for something in the refrigerator, or rifling through a cabinet, or whatever, when I let myself out. You didn't commit a crime, and the only crime I committed was theft in the interest of insuring that my colleague's rights were respected." I said and leaned back in the booth, satisfied with the plan I had concocted.

"You're asking me to lie to the Department of the Interior?"

Her expression twisted into one of disgust. It was as if I had personally offended her.

"There aren't any victims here. Once this is over, I'll be back at work like nothing happened and so will you. You'll never have to see me again."

She averted her eyes. She didn't want to look at me.

"Lying to the State is wrong, Marlow."

She shook her head and stared at the floor. I closed my eyes for a moment and took a few deep breaths to suppress my frustration. She was correct, but surely, she could see that this crime would be victimless.

"This lie helps everyone including the State. I can better serve the State behind my desk than behind bars, Ashley," I said through clenched teeth.

"I'm sorry, Marlow, I can't do that." She dropped a couple of dollars on the table and slid towards the end of the booth.

"This isn't some hypothetical ethics question," I pleaded. "Do you actually think I have a shred of disloyalty in me? Do you honestly think you're helping Vexrus, or anyone for that matter, by getting me locked up?"

She shook her head, stood, and headed for the door.

"Look at me. You're killing me. You can at least look at me!" I shouted, drawing the attention of the restaurant. I stood, facing her.

"Just stop. I won't mention this conversation, and I'll speak well of you when they come," she said sternly. "But I won't lie."

She hurried out of the diner, leaving me standing with clenched fists. I looked around at the people staring at me. An old woman sitting across the room shook her head, and the people seated next to her whispered to one another. One of the waitresses pulled out her phone and glared at me. I needed to redefine the scene they had just witnessed. If any of them had overheard us and felt the urge to inform the authorities about suspicious behavior, Eleanor's image of me could have been tarnished. I could not produce artificial tears but wiped my eyes in front of them in an attempt to convince them that I was crying.

"I'm sorry you all had to witness my breakup. Please don't let us disrupt your evenings," I announced to the entire restaurant.

I left a substantial tip on the table and left without another word. I heard hushed mumbling as the doors closed behind me. Some of them pitied me, some of them mocked me, some returned to their meals in silence, but no one seemed to think that I had been trying to subvert the justice system.

I returned home and sat down on the couch. Out of sheer exhaustion, I fell asleep almost immediately. I slept for nearly ten hours, waking up around seven o'clock the next day. I ate some forgotten stale bread and weighed my options. It was unlikely that Ashley had been contacted in the time since our meeting. She was probably still asleep, meaning that I had some time to find a solution. I turned on the shower and felt the alcohol-scented sweat pour off of me down the drain. My thoughts were scattered from the constant stress of proving that I was a good person to the State. I had no method of contacting Ashley aside from a payphone, and I doubted that she would meet with me again. The only thing that mattered was convincing Ashley to lie for me. My afterlife now depended on this. I couldn't threaten her; if I did, she would be placed under State protection until I had been arrested. Trying to convince Eleanor to not interrogate Ashley would likely prompt her to do so sooner. I briefly considered paying Ashley, but good citizens were unbribable. No one in the nation was dumb enough to trade their soul for money; that behavior was relegated to cartoon villains. I dried off, brushed my teeth, and pulled a jumpsuit out of my closet. I had planned on going to work that day to explain myself to my bosses, but doing so would not have improved my situation. I stuffed every coin in my apartment into my pockets and jogged down the street to the payphone to call Ashley again. I dropped a coin in and dialed her number.

"Hello?" she answered.

"It's Marlow. Remember our talk yesterday? If you could just reconsider your answer, I'm sure I could make it worth your while. Name your price," I pleaded despite having no faith in the power of bribery in Visryan.

"No, Marlow," she said and hung up the phone.

I launched a barrage of obscenities at the payphone and inserted another coin. She picked up, but I heard only silence.

"Hello?" I said and heard a click on the other end. She had hung up on me.

I sprinted down the sidewalk until I saw another payphone, one with a number that she would not immediately recognize, and dialed her number again. It rang a few times before she answered.

"Stop ignoring me! My life depends on this."

"No, now leave me alone." She hung up again.

I emptied a pocket's worth of coins into the machine but was ignored every time. I bashed the phone against the machine until it cracked, after which I simply sat down against the wall. With that bridge burned, I focused on damage control. Impersonating a member of the Department of the Interior, failure to turn heretical materials over to the State, in the worst-case scenario, heresy— I would face thirty years of hard labor and die well before earning enough afterlife credit to ascend. I would be sentenced to damnation, but I would live in fear of death for a few years beforehand. I had to reduce my sentence to something survivable. The dust and fumes in the mines kill most of the incarcerated after four or five years, assuming that an accident does not kill them sooner. Labor such as this was reserved for crimes against the State. Criminals who committed egregious acts that did not pertain to the State were sent to less-cruel labor camps that often focused on reeducation followed by processing raw materials or harvesting crops. I would be miserable but alive. I could work for twenty years or so and still qualify for heaven.

It was then that I realized what must be done in order to avoid oblivion. A single witness had the ability to end me and no one else. The person that had set this sequence of events into motion, the person who refused to help me. I would stop Ashley from incriminating me by committing a crime worthy of such a labor camp: murder. She would ascend to heaven, and I would have the chance to do the same. Heretics were unable to serve the State, but a murderer could be rehabilitated and work to further Visryan's goals in the name of Vexrus. To have a chance at proving myself to the State and entering heaven, I had to kill Ashley.

Chapter 7

I didn't *want* to kill her. I dreaded committing such a horrendous act. I scoured my mind for a way to convince her to lie to Eleanor, but Ashley's devotion was unwavering. I had to bury my trepidation. I had been backed into a corner. Either she was going to heaven or both of us were. Part of me felt anger towards the State. Visryan's policies forced my hand. I was incentivized to become a murderer. What remained of her earthly life paled in comparison to the perfect eternity that awaited her, but my eternity was far from guaranteed. She could have simply agreed to go along with my story; instead, she chose to become an obstacle to my ascension. And for what—adherence to State regulations regardless of whether or not they benefited the nation? Had she agreed to help me, I could have been at work enjoying the rest of my life.

By now, Ashley might have gone to the authorities and told them what I had done to lessen her punishment. Her crime was minor and could likely have been absolved entirely if she helped the Department of the Interior to convict me. I would be arrested, of that I was certain. I would be dragged through the same filth Reggie had been, and gunned down before an audience regardless of my belief. If she survived my assault, or if I were arrested on my way to her apartment, I would choose her to be my witness. I wanted her to look me in the eyes when they killed me. When *she* killed me. If I succeeded, I would blame her. I would tell the courts that she deliberately gave me those banned materials and that the hatred they inspired drove me to kill her. My friendship with her drove me to lie to the State, but my love for Visryan prevailed and sparked a murderous rage in me. A healthy rage aimed at those who defied the State. The extremely faithful jury they would choose for me would be sympathetic. This course of action would not endanger Ashley; by the time her reputation was ruined, she would be rejoicing with the omnipotent. If I presented this case and my otherwise exemplary record to a judge, they would grant me a chance to earn my afterlife back. Regardless of how I would be required to debase myself in the near future, I knew that my best chance for mercy would be to stop Ashley from talking with Eleanor or testifying against me. If she were not able to testify, I could control the narrative.

I figured that killing her would be easy enough. I could overpower her and bash her head in with whatever debris I could find in the street along the way. I would not care who witnessed the attack. I was going to prison regardless. My goal was to avoid the firing squad. Until she was dead, I was dead. The people in the hallway would stare at me in shock. They would scream for the police and drown the emergency services in panicked phone calls. Once she was dead, I would march outside, liberated from death once again and eager to serve the State and its deity. Sirens would blare and flashing blue lights would encircle me. Red dots borne from a dozen rifles would dance across my vital spots, and I would let my weapon fall to the pavement. The agents that arrested me would call me a monster, unaware that the State itself had forced me to commit murder.

As I passed by a dumpster, a gray piece of metal caught my eye. I knelt down to investigate and found a piece of pipe about the length of my forearm. This would suffice. I slid it into my jumpsuit pocket and continued onward. The agent watching me from a parked car or the roof of a nearby building must have been concerned. They may have even been calling for backup or staring at the side of my head through the scope of a rifle. Whether I was to be shot on the way to her apartment or face her testimony in a courtroom, the result would have been the same: oblivion. I walked unbothered by the threat of a government observer. Surely, they were watching me. Be it an agent from a window or an engineer operating a camera on a satellite, they were watching me. I envisioned how Eleanor's conversation with Ashley would go. When offered complete exoneration in exchange for providing evidence against me, she would drop to her knees and thank Vexrus and the State for their mercy.

I flung the doors to her housing complex open and walked to the elevator. The people scattered around the entrance stepped aside to let me in without paying me much attention. A couple of children brushed past me and ran outside. I selected Ashley's floor and rode with an old man staring into space. None of these people knew who I was, nor did they have any reason to. But by the time the nightly news aired, everyone in Relis would know my name. Murders were rare, especially those that sparked an investigation by the Department of the Interior. This crime could demand the attention of media outlets across the nation. There would be factions that believed me to be guilty, but there would also be a considerable population that saw me as the victim. Scholars would point to me as an example of why one should avoid banned materials. The old man exited on the floor below Ashley's. He mumbled something to me before he left, but I did not hear him. The adrenaline flooding my system gave me tunnel vision. My every thought revolved around the coming minutes.

I stepped out of the elevator and into an isolated hallway. I heard the muffled laughter of housewives and their children through several of the doors as I passed by. I figured that it must have been about ten o'clock. This worked to my benefit. The only people able to swarm the hallway when they heard the screams would be mothers, children, and the infirm. I was confident that I could complete the act uncontested. I stood facing Ashley's door under a flickering fluorescent light, knocked twice, and called her name.

"Ashley, it's Marlow. The Department of the Interior wants to question us together." I waited for a moment and watched for movement behind the peephole in the door. I knocked again. "This is serious. Come on, open up." I heard nothing but the buzzing light above my head and the laughter of a woman watching television next door. I slammed my fist against the wood with enough force to silence her neighbors. "Ashley, are you there?" I leaned against the door. "It's really important that you open up now, Ashley. I promise you don't want to ignore me." Again, no response. I considered the possibility that she may not have been home, or worse, that she had already been arrested or sought State protection, but the sound of glass shattering on tile through the wooden door assuaged this fear. "I can hear you, Ashley. Come take a look at the man you're killing!"

I rattled the doorknob and was surprised that it would turn. She must have panicked and hidden somewhere in her apartment to call the police without remembering to lock the door. I pulled the pipe from my pocket and entered, holding it above my head ready to bludgeon her. When I stepped inside, I was elated to see that her lights were left on. She was here, and afraid. I closed the door behind me and locked it.

The layout of her apartment mimicked mine as did essentially all one-person apartments in the city. I entered into a living area that led into a short hallway connected to a kitchen, then a bathroom followed by a single bedroom. I looked behind her chair and under the couch and found nothing. I then crept into the kitchen. I held my breath so that I could better hear hers. I felt glass crunch under my shoe; she had knocked a vase off of the kitchen counter when she heard me. I swapped the pipe to my left hand a picked up a kitchen knife with my right. If she were curled up in a cabinet, stabbing would be a more tactical approach. I knelt down and opened one cabinet door after another, moving quietly so that I could hear footsteps behind me. I swung each door open and thrust the knife into thin air. After doing little more than scuffing pots and pans, I stood and walked to the bathroom. I opened the door and saw nothing remarkable save for a full tub. A rolled-up towel sat at one end of the tub accompanied by a few lit scented candles. I crept over to it and swirled my fingers around in the water. It was still slightly warm. A trail of water droplets let back into the hallway. I had caught her off guard. I returned to the hallway and looked at my silhouette against her stark-white bedroom door, the knife in one hand and the pipe in the other.

"Ashley, I let myself in. I hope that's alright. Come on out so we can get this over with. I would hate for the State to have to use force."

I stood inches from her door and waited for her to open it, or at least crack it a little. She would press her face against the slit, and in that instant, I would kick it in and stab her.

"Come on now, be a good citizen."

Fed up with being ignored by my killer, I slammed my foot against the door, and it flew open. The doorknob left a sizable dent in the drywall.

"You did this to me! I was a good citizen. I served my country; I did my time. We could have both walked away if you hadn't fucked me over! You're lucky. After I crack your head open, you'll be going to heaven."

I marched into her room prepared to commit murder. Her bed was unmade. I stabbed the wads of fabric thinking that she might be hidden but heard no screams. Aside from dust and photo albums, I found nothing under the bed. There was no furniture to hide behind in her bedroom, but there was a closet. Its doors hung slightly open, and the light was off. The tail of her bath towel poked out of the dark. I sauntered to it, finally satisfied that I had found my killer.

"You've ruined my life and maybe even my afterlife, Ashley."

I stood in front of the closet, expecting to hear begging, or be attacked, but it remained still and quiet.

"What, you can't even address me?" I grew angrier standing still on the outside looking at the hanging clothes before me. "Say my name. Say the name of the man you killed!"

I flipped the light switch and tore her clothes from their hangers to reveal a curled-up form crying softly in the corner. She looked up at me and shook her head. She blubbered pleas for mercy, but regardless of whether or not I pitied her, she *needed* to die. Ashley was not stupid. She knew exactly why I was going to kill her. There was no need to explain myself. I saw fear in her puffy, tear-filled eyes, but not the same fear I had. Hers was instinctual, given to her by millions of years of evolution. Mine was deeper. Mine was borne of a concept unknown to those who have never questioned their faith. I envied her. She would never know of the dread that haunted me. The horror before her would last only minutes and be followed by paradise. She could not possibly sympathize with me, and part of me hated her for it.

"I'm not a bad person, Ashley. I don't want to be here, but you left me no choice."

She was not listening. This moment overwhelmed her as it would have overwhelmed me had I not been exposed to the thought of oblivion.

"I will dedicate myself to the State after this. I will serve god in everything that I do. I don't want to do this, but you, or rather Visryan, forced me to."

She looked terrified. For a moment, I hesitated. Such barbarism repulsed me. On the floor above us and in the hallway outside, I could hear panicked murmuring. I wasn't going to walk out of this building a free man. The next time I would stand unshackled would likely be in a courtroom, and if I were to win my case, she needed to be absent. I slammed the pipe against the side of her head and blood splattered across the wall. Anyone on her floor would have heard the screaming. Eleanor may have been listening to us from the hallway as she was preparing her questions for Ashley. The subsequent blows elicited sickening squishing sounds from her shattered skull. I know not how many times I hit her, but I continued well after the screaming stopped. Her corpse slid down the wall and collapsed in front of me, still twitching. I backed away from it and tossed the pipe and knife across the room. In the pursuit of once again becoming a good citizen, I had killed a good citizen.

Within a minute, blue light filled her bedroom as police cars encircled the building. They would soon arrive to drag me away. I walked to her bathroom and saw myself crying and trembling in the mirror. Blood and chunks of brain matter covered me head to toe. I took her hand towel and wiped my face. I kept saying to myself that Vexrus knew that I was a good citizen. I told myself that sending her to paradise before she could be charged with anything was an act of mercy. This way, we could both enter heaven. I managed to give myself a smile before returning to the living room and sitting on her couch. The sound of boots on wood grew steadily louder. The door rattled on its hinges as an agent of the State pressed against it. One of them shouted something before shattering the lock with their boot.

They stormed in and surrounded me. A dozen officers in black body armor swept every inch of the apartment in seconds. Five people fanned out in front of me, each pointing a rifle at my head.

"What happened here? Identify yourself. Are you armed? Are you the tenant? If not, what is your relationship with the tenant?"

One of them paused and pressed a button on what I assumed to have been a microphone on the side of his helmet and the questioning ended. Outside, I heard neighbors telling agents the identity of the resident followed by soft crying. Two of them emerged from the bedroom with their guns trained on me. The one closest to me grabbed me by my collar and pulled me upright.

"You're under arrest for the murder of Ashley Davis," one of them said. I remained silent and placed my hands behind my back. "If you voluntarily confess, provide us with any information you believe to be useful, and answer all of our questions to the best of your ability, the record of your arrest will reflect it. Do you understand?" I felt cold metal handcuffs click into place behind me as he spoke.

"Yes sir, I understand. My name is Marlow Wilson, and I killed Ashley Davis."

A team of medical professionals carted a stretcher to her bedroom. I felt one of the officers press a handgun into my back and grip the handcuff chain.

"We're going outside. Please walk forward."

I obeyed, and walked escorted by police on either side. As I passed through the door, I saw the medics returning with a corpse in a body bag. I could not help but smile as the last shreds of uncertainty dissipated. I had a concrete chance to enter eternity. Every onlooker I passed scowled at me. A bawling old woman glared in disgust at the smiling murderer in front of her. Their hatred mattered little. I would one day be forgiven for this crime and join all of them in the kingdom of heaven. There would be no more suffering for any of us fifty years from then.

We rode down the elevator in silence. There was nothing to say; I had already confessed and would eagerly comply with any demand. When the doors opened on the bottom floor, I was met with a familiar face: Eleanor. She pulled a badge from her uniform's breast pocket and showed it to the police officers.

"Eleanor Riley, Department of the Interior. This man is the subject of an active investigation, and I will be taking him into custody."

She ordered a pair of agents, one man and one woman, to take me to a vehicle parked in front of the housing complex. Her warm expression had been replaced by an intense scowl. The woman I had placed my trust in was nowhere to be found. I looked away from her. She had shown me mercy, and my actions had caused her trouble. I hoped that she would not be demoted or fired. She stood still in front of the elevator glaring at me until the doors closed behind me. The person I thought to be my ally had become an enemy, and everyone I knew would now see me as a criminal, but I could not stop smiling.

Chapter 8

They shackled my arms and legs and strapped me into the back seat of an armored van. The doors slammed shut and were locked from the outside. The sunlight beaming through the bars on the windows cast a grid pattern across me. Many of the once-friendly faces I saw on Vexrus Day looked at me in disbelief from outside of the van. Camera crews capturing what footage of me they could lined the opposite side of the street. A few reporters pressed against the side of the van to take pictures. Their questions were muffled by the thick glass and armor plating. I saw Eleanor leave the building surrounded by journalists. She stared at the ground and pushed the microphones away from her face as she walked. She shook her head and said something to her male subordinate, who then blocked their advances. Her eyes met mine though the bullet-proof glass. The anger I had seen at the bottom of the elevator had been replaced by disappointment. She motioned to the female subordinate, who walked around the back of the van and entered the driver seat. She then entered, followed by the other.

"So, where to now Captain Ellie?" the one behind in the driver's seat asked.

"The courthouse hopefully followed by Harold's, and I don't think you have to call me captain anymore," she said as the other subordinate patted her on the back.

"I'll vouch for you. You're a great captain; no one could have predicted this." he said in a consoling tone, glaring at me out of the corner of his eye.

"I appreciate it, Devin, but I'm honestly not too upset about a demotion. After all, I deserve one. Had I arrested him immediately, he would never have killed anyone." She looked back at me. "Some people are irredeemable."

She turned forward again and went silent. Everyone watching the van pass by, everyone that was going to watch the nightly news, and everyone sitting in front of me thought that I was irredeemable, but the State in its infinite mercy had yet to give up on me.

"What's going to happen to me? Am I going to a reeducation camp?" I asked.

"After you're found guilty, you'll be going to Martyr Harold's Labor Camp where you'll work off your crime. It houses those who commit crimes against the State as well as those who commit severe crimes while under investigation. You know, the type of crime one might commit to hinder our ability to gather evidence." She watched the crowds of onlookers as we passed by them. "I know why you did it. You can tell the investigators whatever you want. In fact, I know that's the point, but both you and I know why you did it."

"Could you hear inside her apartment? I asked."

"No. We did not believe it to be necessary, but I wish we had."

I could not help but breathe a sigh of relief.

"You're garbage, Marlow. If it were up to me, I would put a bullet in your head right now, but I don't believe in subverting the State's justice system, unlike you. Hopefully, Vexrus will kill you before your debt can be paid. Maybe he will give another prisoner a vision instructing them to beat you to death like you did to Ashley Davis."

She was right, but had no proof. No one could prove my motive as long as I kept my story straight. I had successfully subverted the Department of the Interior and the legal system.

"That patch sewn onto your uniform doesn't make you smarter than everyone around you," I said. "Stop preaching at me. You don't know a goddamn thing about me."

I wanted to explain myself. I hated letting the woman who had faith in me suffer through such guilt.

"You haven't won yet, Marlow." She turned around and glared at me. "I'll be testifying at the trial, and you can't kill me like you did Ashley."

She turned forward again and went silent. I thought it best to not antagonize her for the rest of the trip; after all, she wanted me dead and had the means to make it so. I watched a horde of military police rush into my building as we passed it. They would not find anything of use as Eleanor had already taken everything, but part of me still felt violated. Under any other set of circumstances, I would never have done something so heinous, and was angry that the State's afterlife system had forced my hand. They were raiding a good citizen's house and dragging his name through the mud. After twenty minutes of driving in silence, we reached the Relis Courthouse. Journalists crowded around the van snapping pictures of me and a couple of a frustrated Eleanor. The court's security pulled them aside and cleared a drivable path. Within thirty minutes, my crime had become the latest sensation. These leeches vegetated on police scanners seven days a week waiting for something like this to sate their thirst. Before the trial began, their headlines would make me lose in the court of public opinion and, more importantly, unemployable, impeding my ability to accrue afterlife credit.

We pulled into a garage and, with the flip of a switch, we were sealed off from the outside. Eleanor and her team exited the vehicle and spoke with an official for a few minutes before an agent of the court walked to the back of the van. The locking mechanism groaned, and the double doors opened. He yelled something to another guard who joined him. They each grabbed ahold of one of my shoulders and the horizontal chain between my arms, and pulled me out of the van. They kept holding onto the chain and motioned to a door on the other side of the room.

"We're gonna walk you through that door and to a holding cell where you'll be given an attorney and time to prepare for court proceedings. If you comply, this will all go smoothly," one of them said and pushed me forward.

I nodded and did as I was told. I stepped into a white room lined with cells behind thick steel doors. Each one had a small slit for a window and judging by where I was located in the building, they would be my only view outside. I was ushered through a door labeled "prisoner orientation" located next to the cells, where I was met with another staff member. She had an emotionless expression and sorted through boxes of supplies on a rack behind her desk. I was thrilled to see someone with what appeared to be a neutral image of me instead of a furious officer or invasive journalist. One of the guards removed my chains and brandished a pistol which I took as a reminder to stay put.

"Strip down and put these on and put your clothes and anything you brought with you on the desk. In the case that you are found innocent, they will all be returned to you," she said in a disinterested tone.

She plopped a neon green jumpsuit in front of me along with a pair of underwear and malleable rubber shoes. I looked over my shoulder at the guards and sighed. I did as I was instructed and changed in front of them. My new clothes were itchy and slightly too large. I started to ask for a smaller size, but she spoke before I could.

"Your number is nine-three-eight." She pointed at a tag just below the collar of my uniform with the same numbers on it. "You'll be given more suits of clothing as well as grooming supplies within the next day or two. These men will escort you to your new home."

She stuffed my belongings into a bag, and they disappeared behind the desk. The guards turned me around and walked me to a cell just outside of her office. One of them swiped a plastic card through a reader next to the cell and the lock unlatched.

"Do you have a lawyer you'd like us to contact?" one of them asked as I stepped inside.

"No."

Though an expensive, well-trained lawyer may have been able to get me a lighter sentence, I felt that a short trial with a remorseful defendant might placate Eleanor as well as the rest of the Department of the Interior.

"One will be assigned to you, then. You'll get your meals through this hatch here three times a day." He jiggled the hatch a little and excused himself from the room, leaving me alone.

In my room, there was a sink, toilet, and small bed with a copy of *The Book of Vexrus* laying on it. I wondered if it had been placed there by Eleanor to taunt me, but it was far more likely that they were given to all prisoners. As expected, my view was limited to the tiny window facing the entrance area. I would spend the next days, weeks, or maybe months of my life watching guards carry out their daily duties. In the corner of my cell near the door, I saw a piece of rounded black glass. They were monitoring me. I had not expected jail cells of the yet-to-be-found-guilty to be under constant surveillance, especially considering that there was a window facing staff members going about their business. I thought it to be unlikely, but I worried that they were placed there by the Department of the Interior. In the event that it was, I needed to avoid incriminating statements or anything indicative of unacceptable thought. I looked over to *The Book of Vexrus* on my bed. If prisoner recordings were to be used in the trial, footage of me constantly reading the sacred book may work in my favor. I reclined on my bed and opened the book at such an angle that the camera would be unable to follow my eyes. I had no interest in reading the book as I already believed in its message and the State and had read through it several times. Because of Reggie, the book in my hands filled me with disgust and anxiety despite its cosmic significance. I envied those who had never read or understood it but believed every word. The State and thus Vexrus never punished them for being uneducated; instead, it celebrated their unwavering faith. I resolved to be one of them after my sentence. I would never question the divine mysteries of the book, nor would I read new versions. The focus of my existence would be the afterlife number displayed on a computer screen.

I stared blankly at the book until night fell and the lights turned off. The camera could not see me in the dark, so there was no need to continue clutching the book. I tossed it onto the floor and crawled into bed. The pillow and sheets were surprisingly soft. Until one was sentenced, it seemed that the State took care of the imprisoned. Once the chattering guards left and the constant opening and closing of doors ceased, I was left in silence. There was no view outside of my tiny window, only absolute darkness. As the night wore on, I heard groaning outside of my cell across the room that slowly metamorphosed into wailing. Though the majority of what he said was unintelligible, I managed to gather that he had been charged with heresy. I, as well as most of the people I knew, was under the impression that heresy was a rare crime. Good citizens never questioned Vexrus or the State and doing so was indicative of immorality or a mental illness. If there had been a heretic arrested in my district of Relis, it would have been discussed on the news or announced with wanted posters like Reggie, assuming that the Department of the Interior did not remedy the situation beforehand. I saw a sliver of light cut through the room outside to the door across from mine. I knelt down beside my window and watched as a guard shined a flashlight into the neighboring heretic's cell. He pushed the hatch below the window open and said something inaudible to the man.

There was a pause followed by constant screaming. Whatever the guard said had inspired nightmarish fear in the prisoner. Two more guards then joined the first, and they entered his cell together. After thirty seconds of screaming and gargling, the room went silent again.

Had they killed him? Perhaps they had given him sedatives to calm him down so that the rest of the prisoners could sleep. One of them shined his flashlight around the room looking into the cells. I ducked under the window and watched as a beam of light shone onto my bed and disappeared. The way that my sheets had been arranged may have fooled him into thinking that I was in bed; after all, he only saw into my cell for an instant. I pressed my face against the door and brought my eye up to the lower right corner. He was inspecting each cell more closely. I retreated from the door and crawled across the floor to my bed. I could hear his boots against the tile outside as he drew closer. I slid into bed and pulled the sheets over myself, my back facing the door. Light bounced off of the back wall and around my cell as he inspected it. I squeezed my eyes shut as the spotlight rested on me. He kept it there for a few seconds before walking to the next cell. If they were simply calming him down, why would they feel the need to inspect inside the quiet cells?

I lay in bed for at least half an hour trying to remain absolutely motionless. Once I believed it to be safe, I rolled over as naturally as I could manage, and watched my window. The outside was dark again; I believe it had been dark for a while by then. I stared at it for what seemed like hours. In absolute darkness and in the absence of a clock, gauging the passage of time was difficult. A flashlight appeared once again at least a couple of hours after the initial incident. A pair of guards returned to the cell across from me, but I could not discern what they were doing from my bed. One of them walked out dragging something behind him and disappeared from view. The other closed the cell door and shined his flashlight on the ground behind the first guard. Light reflected off of the floor and leaked through the hatch under my window. I stared at it for a moment before realizing that my hatch had been left partially open. I may have been the only prisoner that heard him. The soundproofing on his cell made him nearly indiscernible. His wails could not have penetrated two sets of doors. The way that the beds were situated almost guaranteed that his flashlight could not shine in anyone's face and awaken them be accident. It would have only shined onto their backs or torsos. As I watched the last one vanish, I realized that the thin windows prevented prisoners from seeing more than the three cells across from theirs. I may have been the sole witness to whatever transpired that night.

Chapter 9

At some point that night, I managed to fall asleep. I awoke around mid-morning, and the view outside of my cell was the same as the day before save for the empty cell across from me. Whatever I saw had not interrupted business as usual. I glanced up at the camera in the corner. It would not have been able to see me when I was up against the door, but it may have caught sight of my empty bed when he illuminated it. I heard a metallic clang as a tray of breakfast food slid through the hatch. I got out of bed, grabbed it, and thanked the guard. Immediately after, the hatch slammed shut and my room became silent. This confirmed my suspicion. In any case, the tactical thing to do would be to appear as inconspicuous as possible for the camera. I sat on the floor and forced myself to eat rock-hard toast and dry scrambled eggs without looking up from my tray. Afterwards, I washed my hands and resumed sitting on my bed and staring at a page from *The Book of Vexrus*.

Around noon, shortly after an unpleasant lunch consisting of fatty pork and watery baked beans, a guard opened my cell and informed me that I would be meeting with a public defender after a shower. I placed my hands behind my back to be handcuffed and, once my bindings clicked into place, we walked down a hallway on the right side of the room outside of my cell. Before turning into the hallway, I analyzed the room to the best of my ability. I had paid little attention when they first brought me in; after all, I had expected to be there for only a short time before being shipped off to life in a labor camp. Since I had confessed to murder at the scene of the crime, I anticipated only a short trial in which I would express my guilt and regret, followed by a sentencing, and be finished. But if the State intended to try me for impersonating a member of the Department of the Interior or even heresy instead of murder, I may have had to live there for longer than expected. I glanced around the room as we walked and counted the cells. There were five along my wall, with mine being in the middle. Five cells also lined the opposite wall. Two sat on either side of the door through which I entered, and no cells occupied the other wall. Instead, there was the hallway down which I was being led, the office of the woman I had spoken with one day earlier, and a set of double doors that led to parts unknown. Only four of the cells were occupied, counting myself. I knew that Visryan's crime rate was low, but only four people were being held in the jail of one of the busiest sections of a major city— though, to be fair, one day earlier there had been five. Every inch of the area was under constant surveillance. A camera sat in every corner and above every doorway, as well as on the ceiling of the hallway at regular intervals. The guard kept me close to the wall. A red line running along the floor separated me from passing staff members. With such a small number of convicts, it was likely that everyone being held was constantly monitored by guards. In a large prison, their attention would have been divided, but I enjoyed no such luxury.

He led me to a small washroom where prisoners were to wash themselves under the eye of the cameras. He handed me a bag of toiletries and allowed me the dignity of make-believe privacy while I cleaned myself. I would have to make my peace with the cameras considering that I would be living under similar conditions until at least my late forties; so, I took my time and cleaned thoroughly. Once finished, he led me further down the hall and into a cramped room with a dented metallic desk in the center accompanied by two chairs. He took out a handcuff key and ordered me to turn around.

"I'm taking off your restraints but behave yourself. This room is being monitored, and, if you try to hit the lawyer or escape, I promise you'll be killed within thirty seconds." he said.

I nodded in agreement and walked inside. As he said, I was being watched. Cameras sat in each corner of the room as well as one under the table.

"Your lawyer will be in shortly. Just sit and wait for him."

He closed the door and locked it from the outside. I sat down on a surprisingly chilly metal seat and looked around my tiny concrete box. This room was even smaller than the one in which Reggie had been killed but enjoyed the same dank and musty atmosphere. The metal furniture was bolted down, presumably to stop a prisoner from turning a chair into a bludgeon. I heard a click through the steel door, and it groaned open to reveal a smiling young man in a suit and tie holding two cups of coffee.

"Hi there. My name is Franklin Bradford, and I'll be representing you."

He strode in and gave me a beaming white smile. He slid one of the cups of coffee over to me and began pulling files out of a satchel. This man's presence bolstered my confidence considerably. He looked like a hybrid between a lawyer and a salesman. Surely, this man could improve my image in the eyes of the Department of the Interior as well as the public.

"Nice to meet you, Franklin. As I'm sure you already know, my name is Marlow."

"You can call me Frank," he said while shaking my hand. "Now let's get down to business. First thing's first: do you believe in and are willing to die for the truth contained in *The Book of Vexrus* and the State over which Vexrus rules?"

"I do, and I am," I responded.

"Do you swear that you are in no way a heretic?"

"I do."

"Excellent, now let's prepare our argument."

He slid a stack of pictures in front of me almost immediately. The one on top must have been taken at the crime scene. It showed a battered, nude Ashley sprawled out in front of police officers. Even one's attorney was required to denounce them as a heretic if they believed them to be one. Regular crimes were granted a measure of client-attorney privilege, but heresy was an exception. It was for this reason that he asked me to swear to those statements, and I suspected it was also for this reason that he was forcing these photographs in front of me without warning. He as well as someone watching through the cameras wanted to see my reaction. I was being tried before my trial, as all potential heretics were. The State believed heretics to be necessarily morally deficient and thus unable to express guilt correctly. If I could convince this man of my piety, or display the necessary qualities for him to say that I had, he would become my greatest ally. Though, it was possible that the Department of the Interior had already turned him against me. This was the first time since the murder that I had been forced to face what I had done. I felt intense emotion staring at the photos, but needed to be cognizant of how I presented myself. Part of me wanted to tell Frank the truth, the whole truth, but under such circumstances even my lawyer could not be trusted. I buried my face in my hands and sighed.

"You confessed already, right?" Frank said.

"Yeah, I did it. I was just so angry about the books, and I snapped. I didn't want to hurt anybody," I said, whimpering and rubbing my eyes in an attempt to artificially redden them.

He watched for any sign of improper thought, as did whoever was behind the cameras. He scribbled something down on a notepad before patting me on the shoulder.

"I'm sure you were. I'd be angry, too."

I doubt that he cared whether or not I was telling the truth. He needed to look like he believed me in order to be my attorney. My case was likely going to be a high-profile one, considering Visryan's low crime rate and the popularity of heresy trials, and it could raise his profile substantially.

"We'll make sure you still get to the afterlife. I guarantee it," he said.

I maintained my dejected expression for a few minutes longer in view of the cameras before returning to normal. He ignored me while sifting through his pile of documents and arranging them on the table. We had successfully gone through the motions of the client-lawyer relationship and could now discuss the matter at hand.

"Do you understand what exactly this trial is going to be, Marlow? They think that you killed Ashley to cover up evidence of your lack of faith. If we're lucky, you'll walk out of that room seen as a murderer."

I had killed her to cover up my impersonating a member of the Department of the Interior: a severe infraction punishable by years of labor and a substantial reduction in afterlife credit, not heresy, which carried an even greater penalty. Eleanor had accused me of being subhuman! I had been slandered as an immoral degenerate who was incapable of being a good citizen.

"A heretic? The State thinks that I'm a heretic. Are they insane? Hell, faith is what made me kill her in the first place!" I shouted.

I slammed my fists on the table and glared at Franklin. "Do you think that?"

"No, of course not. What you said makes perfect sense to me, and I'm sure it will make perfect sense to a jury."

He showed me pictures of shattered electronics on my apartment floor. Cracked plastic screens and exposed wires surrounded the nearly empty vodka bottle from that hellish night.

"You went crazy when your faith was stolen from you and took it out on Ashley, since she gave you the books. As science tells us, a lack of faith would affect anyone's judgment. Though I do need to know why you took those books from her in the first place. Did she give them to you?"

"Yes, my colleague, Reginald Finster, had gotten them from somewhere and was executed for disseminating banned materials, among other things. I was his witness. When he was supposed to make his final statement, one of the guards pulled out a piece of paper and read aloud a stilted, cookie-cutter fake. This was illegal, as I'm sure you're aware, and prompted me to investigate. Then, when I was at Ashley's apartment a month or so later, she requested that I dispose of Reggie's belongings for her. I agreed and left. The books made me question my faith, setting this whole thing into motion. I was merely trying to ensure that the State's civil institutions were functioning properly and got in over my head."

There was no need to protect Ashley now. Why serve an additional sentence for theft when blaming her would have no consequences for either one of us?

"The Department of the Interior is under the impression that they were stolen from her."

"I said that to protect Ashley, but later realized that my wavering faith had altered my judgment, making me lie to the State and further contributing to the anger that led me to kill her."

He narrowed his eyes for a moment. Perhaps I had come off as too self-aware. Should I have demonstrated such an understanding of my own mental state given the angry confusion from which I had professed to suffer? He nodded slightly and turned his attention back towards the contents of his satchel.

"Okay, understood." He flipped through a stack of papers from the Department of Public Spending. "Your record, aside from recent events of course, is fantastic. Proving your piety will be a breeze."

My subtle interrogation had come to an end. Though he would undoubtedly continue searching for signs of wavering faith. Faith in Vexrus was performative, and the performance continued unceasing from cradle to grave.

Though it seemed that I might have to confess to lying to Eleanor, the plan was working. If I could frame myself as the victim, I could be free after fifteen years. Ashley weakened my faith, and I struck back. My story could have inspired a movie. Regardless of what Eleanor thought, I was going to be a good person. We spent hours discussing blood splatters on the floor and the weapon I had used. To the best of my ability, I recalled every word that I had said to Eleanor, and we found no glaring weakness in our case. Despite her posturing, neither she nor the Department of the Interior could damage me. A heresy trial was an unattainable dream for them. I was guilty of lying to the State, murder, theft, and impersonation, but I was no heretic. The only charges they would be able to stick would be lying to the State about how I obtained the books, and murder. Severe crimes to be sure, but not ones that would threaten my eternity. I returned to my cell confident that the system would exonerate me and restore me to my rightful, guaranteed afterlife status.

I stared at the sacred book until lights-out and crawled into bed. There were no sounds or movements to observe. I was alone in complete blackness. The images Frank had shown me crept into the back of my mind. My desperation had numbed me, but now I had all the time in the world to ruminate on what I had done. I'm sure Ashley had a family. Perhaps they would be present at the trial. I wanted to atone for my crime, but how could I? Speaking the truth carried with it a far more severe penalty than death. Part of my punishment would be the grating guilt gnawing at my mind for the remainder of my earthly life. I worried that the State would levy some sort of post-mortem punishment on her if they thought she contributed to the dissemination of banned materials. For what must have been hours, I begged Vexrus to save her from oblivion. I eventually fell into a restless sleep. I wondered if I would ever sleep soundly again.

I spent the following week locked in a rigid schedule. I ate when instructed to and washed when instructed to. Frank and I formulated arguments and retorts for every circumstance we could conceive of. If the Department of the Interior were to inquire about any minute facet of my life, I wanted to have a three-page-long statement about it to turn to. During every waking moment under the cell camera, I skimmed *The Book of Vexrus*, and, in the darkness, I toiled under my guilty conscience. Frank praised my plan to read the book during my free time and was overjoyed when he found out that I had been doing that before our initial meeting— though, he thought I was actually reading it. If we were lucky, he said, I might only have to serve five years. For every hopeful statement he delivered, he showed me another horrid image or read a vivid description from the investigators. He, or at least his superiors, did not trust me. They kept trying to coax an improper reaction from me, but I maintained my composure. My stomach was in knots, but my somber expression never let on. I wondered if burying my guilt for days on end would give me a stomach ulcer.

Journalists requested to meet with me throughout my stay. Prison officials even recommended that I be interviewed, saying that it could help 'humanize' me to the masses. Thinking it to be a poor strategic decision to speak to the press without a lawyer present, I declined every offer. Media outlets worked hand-in-hand with the Department of the Interior; I could not risk accidentally giving them defamatory footage. I was confident that I was going to win. It felt strange to consider years of imprisonment a victory, but a stint in prison paled in comparison to obliteration.

Chapter 10

I sat in my cell a day before the trial battling the desire to fall asleep while staring at a particularly dull page of the sacred book. To my knowledge, no other strange occurrences had taken place outside of my cell since the first night. Though, my hatch had not been left open since that night, so, I would not have heard anything if there had been any. But I had not seen any flashlights in the night, either. That incident had become a distant memory.

My impending emancipation from death five to fifteen years from then inoculated me to fear of the Department of the Interior. A staff member pushed my hatch open and requested my finished dinner tray. I closed the book and slid the tray through the slot. Moments later, my cell went dark, followed by the room outside. No longer obligated to suffer through *The Book of Vexrus*, I curled up on my tiny bed and watched the staff members' silhouettes as they passed, accented by the slight glow of whatever electronics they were carrying. Light reflected off of the opposing cell's window every time the exit door swung open, bisecting my room with light each time.

Eventually the door stopped opening, and I was left alone in the dark. It had been maybe an hour, and I just began to drift off to sleep, when I saw the familiar beam of light stretch across my room again. I slid down my bed to get a clearer view of them without making any noticeable movements. A trio of silhouettes appeared across the room. I could not hear them, but their body language, or what I could see of it, conveyed that they were talking. A blue light covered them as one of them unlocked their cell phone. My heart sank. Standing in the middle of the trio looking directly into my cell was Eleanor Riley. I remained as still as possible. I feared that she, or another member of the Department of the Interior, had perpetrated the event from six nights prior and intended to subject me to something similar. She was going to subvert the trial and hand me a death sentence before I could argue my case. The group approached my cell, and I rolled onto my side facing away from the door. One of them shined a flashlight through the window and across my bed. I felt around the metal bedframe underneath me searching for a piece that I could break off and use as a weapon, but found nothing.

The light remained on me for minutes. I expected for them to rush into my cell, murder me, and drag me out in a body bag like the apparent heretic across from me. I was unarmed and outnumbered. If they wanted me dead, there was little I could do to stop them. One of them then knocked on my window. I wanted so badly to stay still and prayed for them to leave. I squeezed my eyes shut and gritted my teeth, whispering pleas to Vexrus under my breath. The subsequent knocks grew louder and more insistent. I, thinking it wise to try and negotiate rather than wait for them to enter, relented, and sat upright trying to appear as though I had just awoken. Eleanor stood in front of my window and narrowed her eyes at me. A malevolent grin stretched across her face, and she pushed my hatch open.

"Hello, Marlow. I wanted to tell you in person. The Department of the Interior now has audio from inside Ashley's apartment. Once we told Ashley's cell service provider that we needed help with a heresy case, they were happy to assist us. If your case weren't as public as it is, we would kill and dispose of you, but you get to enjoy the luxury of public humiliation instead. See you in court."

She closed the hatch and walked away with her entourage. The familiar exit-door-light beamed through my window again and vanished, leaving me alone. What exactly had I said to Ashley? Every conversation she had ever had over the phone or within earshot of her phone was going to be entered as evidence. She said my name over the payphone calls, so denying those would prove difficult. Assuming that she had brought her phone when we met at the diner across from her apartment, they had access to enough evidence to convict me of impersonation and lying to the authorities on more than one occasion. Even the lies I had told Frank would be exposed. Depending on how far back the Department of the Interior had searched, they might have audio from when I first received the books. I lay on my back and stared into the darkness above me. My credibility was shattered. We were to deliver opening arguments in less than a day. There was no time to restructure our case or prepare a counter argument. I would have no contact with Frank until just before the trial, and if he thought anything I said was heretical, I would be left to defend myself. I doubted that anything I had said would prove me to be a heretic, but I would be buried under numerous other crimes. Perhaps I deserved such a grim fate. Maybe Vexrus himself saw fit to dangle hope in front of my face and pull it away just as I reached out to grasp it. My crimes would now far exceed taking a peek inside a box filled with banned materials. I felt tears run down my cheeks and was grateful that no one could hear me.

Why would Eleanor tell me? Would it not have been more advantageous to surprise me with the recordings in court? Perhaps the camera in the corner was waiting for a reaction. A scream, a fit of rage, maybe an attempted suicide, whatever would prove that what she said filled me with panic, anything that could be construed as a sign of guilt. She may have just wanted to make my last moments in jail more miserable. I suffered under the camera's gaze for what seemed like an eternity.

The groaning of my hatch awoke me the following morning. I took my breakfast tray, thanked the staff member, and set it on the floor. I then began searching the cell for a place to tie a bedsheet-noose. I wanted to wait until midmorning when the room outside was largely empty and hang myself before the trial, but there was no ceiling fan or hooks in the walls, nor could I fasten a noose to the top of the door. I doubted that I would have had the willpower to take my own life given the opportunity regardless. The paralyzing fear of oblivion had led me to this state, and that fear had only grown stronger. I considered fighting the guards or attempting to run away when they escorted me to the shower, but they would likely subdue me and add "attempted escape" to my growing list of charges. I could have taken Frank hostage and demanded that I be set free, but a partially shackled man wielding the sharpest object in arm's reach would fare poorly against armed guards. If they could manage to tranquilize me instead, I would be forced to endure even worse conditions. It seemed that I would not be able to shed my mortal coil of my own volition, only the State's. I watched staff members and a couple of new prisoners move about outside of my cell. If Eleanor was telling the truth, pretending to read *The Book of Vexrus* no longer served a purpose, nor did hiding problematic behavior from the camera. However, the possibility that she had lied obligated me to continue the farce.

One of the new prisoners looked at me through my cell window and said something to a guard. It seemed that news of my crime had spread around the city, or at least my district. Being a short-term celebrity brought little comfort to me in my four-by-eight cell. A guard approached my cell door and pushed the hatch open.

"Lunch is here. Eat quick; we've got to get you ready for your trial," he said.

I held the hatch open and addressed the guard.

"That guy out there was pointing at me. Does he know who I am?"

The guard looked at me, puzzled.

"Most everyone does. Your trial is going to be broadcast nationally."

I thanked him and took the tray. Despite the fact that my trial being broadcast nationally would ruin my reputation in every part of the country, I actually felt relieved. The State intended to make an example of me. They could not simply make me vanish in the night. The people demanded to see me, and the State had to oblige. My rights would be respected as long as I was on camera. By lifting me up as an example of a bad citizen, Visryan had temporarily guaranteed my safety. Besides, after a long stay in a labor camp, I would likely be unrecognizable to most citizens. They would just see a haggard old man, broken by years of hard work. However, this still assumed that Eleanor was lying.

If Eleanor's recordings were sufficiently incriminating, my trial would end on the first day, and I could be dead and completely obliterated as soon as the next. I choked down as much of my lunch as I could manage before the guards arrived to escort me. Low-grade hotdogs and unimaginably dense bread could have been my last meal. A pair of them opened my cell and instructed me to follow them to the shower. As I stepped out of my cell, I saw the exit door swing open and closed. It did not require a card to open, and I was not bound by any restraints. I wanted to run and hope that their bullets would miss me. Neither of them seemed attentive. Why would they be? I had been nothing short of a model inmate during my brief stay. It would take them a few seconds to draw their guns and take aim. By then, I could be sprinting down the hallway praying that another guard was not approaching from the opposite direction. But I chose to stay, not because my odds of success in the courtroom were greater than my odds of not being shot, but because fleeing would guarantee that I could not, under any circumstances, enter heaven. I still held hope that Vexrus was a merciful god. That hope convinced me that an execution by the State would be preferable to being a damned man on the run. Thanks to Vexrus, those marked for death were obedient in their final moments, standing perfectly still while members of a firing squad took aim.

All I saw on the way from my cell to the transport van were potential escape routes. Outside of the shower, I heard a door creak open down the hallway and saw natural light spill out across the tile. Every staff member that passed by could have been a hostage. I could have reached for one of the guard's weapons and let instinct take over. Even when I believed that the State had abandoned me, faith in Vexrus kept me obedient. I followed every order I was given without protest. When they shackled my legs and cuffed my hands mere feet from an exit, I suppressed the gnawing urge to escape. They must have known how I felt, how every prisoner they sent to their deaths felt. They knew that belief kept us in line, I and the countless others hoping against reason for a way out. These security measures were largely unnecessary; even without them, even if my cell door had been left open, I would never have attempted an escape. A squad of guards strapped me into a chair in the back of a van and connected one of the chains to a hook bolted to the floor next to me.

"You'll change into something presentable when you get there and talk with your lawyer again. It's one o'clock now; the trial starts at three," a guard said before locking me inside.

A reporter across the street was speaking to a camera and pointing at my van. Camera crews from other news stations spilled onto the sidewalk from every direction and filmed me at every angle they could. They must have been watching the prison for hours waiting for an opportunity to glimpse me. A journalist sprinted across the street, microphone in hand, and nearly reached me before a group of guards confronted him. He snapped a few pictures before scurrying back to the rest of his crew. A few guards forced civilians to vacate the road while another cranked the van. As we pulled out onto the road, blue light filled the van from behind. I craned my neck to see a police car following us. Another took its position in front of the van. Evidently, the crowds had become so ravenous that I required a police escort.

People watched us pass by from the streets and their windows. A couple and their children held up signs that said, "rot in oblivion" and "god hates you." The Department of the Interior must have invested a lot in media control for this case. They had probably pumped anti-Marlow propaganda into every household to generate support for more funding, or simply to inspire greater faith in their audience. Public opinion greatly affected heresy trials. The jury would be composed of citizens from my district of the city who were in good standing with the State. By the time the trial began, these people would have been exposed to a feed of constant negative media coverage about me. They would see my face only after reading countless signs calling for me to be torn to shreds in the streets or burned alive. In their minds, I epitomized the secular, hateful, evil of backwards foreigners on their own soil. Frank and I were at a disadvantage. The roadside mob grew as we neared the courthouse. We pulled through a gate which slid closed immediately after. They unshackled me entirely. Both the guards and I knew that I was more likely to survive in custody than in the hands of the crowd.

I was then brought to a small conference room to change and briefly speak with my lawyer before the trial began. Laying across an office chair I saw one of my suits from work, complete with the pin on the breast pocket that labeled me as an employee of the State. Frank must have requested that I wear this suit to counteract my widespread character assassination.

I dressed and waited for Frank. I debated whether or not to tell him about Eleanor's visit. The thought that she may have lied to torment me or prompt me to take my own life still hung in my mind. After all, when I was arrested, she said that the Department of the Interior had not bugged Ashley's apartment. It was still very possible that the trial would proceed exactly as Frank and I had imagined it would. Perhaps the horde of media personnel would enjoy the story of how a cruel person stole a good man's faith and paid the price. I felt a tinge of guilt for dragging Ashley's name through the mud, but at that very moment, she was in ecstasy in heaven unconcerned with worldly things. After all, what good citizen wouldn't trade their reputation for another's salvation?

The door creaking open pulled me from my thoughts. Frank shuffled in, looking down at his shoes with a grave expression on his face.

"Hey, Frank. You're running a bit late; is everything okay?"

He looked up at me and shook his head.

"You son of a bitch. I heard the Department of the Interior's recordings."

He glared at me and clinched his fists at his sides. My chest sank. I swallowed, struggling to maintain my composure. The fear that I had felt when I first read Reggie's books returned. I could hear myself breathing louder. I started to loosen my collar but, worried that Frank was searching for signs of panic, restrained myself.

"What are you talking about? What recordings?"

"Don't lie to me. You know about them. The lady that arrested you, Eleanor I think, sat me down and played nearly an hour of you incriminating yourself. I nearly lost my job just for associating with you."

A drop of sweat slid down the back of my neck. He was undoubtedly wearing a wire, or if there was not a microphone on him, there was one in the room. Despite every primal instinct in my body urging me to run or fight, I had to stand still and watch my tone.

"Look, Frank, I have no idea what you're talking about. I thought you were my lawyer; why are you grilling me instead of our opponents? Besides, this case could mean a lot for your career."

"Marlow, I have a duty to my country. The fact that you would even suggest something like that—well it shows what kind of citizen you are."

I clenched my jaw.

"And what kind of citizen is that?"

I started towards him.

"A monstrous one. One who deserves oblivion. One who is a detriment to the nation," he said, standing his ground.

I looked into his unblinking eyes and felt a tinge of disgust.

"What the fuck do you know about being a good citizen, you parasite? You defend people that you know are guilty for career advancement. Admit it; you thought I was guilty the moment we met."

I leaned down to his chest where I assumed a microphone had been placed.

"If you could, you would still be in my corner pretending we're allies, wouldn't you?!" I shouted.

He staggered back and crossed his arms over his chest confirming my theory.

I understood more than anyone what it felt like to be a faithful citizen in good standing with the State. I could have put a gun to his head, and he would have just stared back at me, unwavering. I tried to think of a way to elicit information about the recordings from him, but nothing could compete with divinity.

"Are you just gonna stand there and yell at me? Confess and accept your punishment. If you're lucky, incredibly lucky, you could be sentenced to fifty or sixty years of labor. That's better than you deserve," he said.

"I have nothing to confess. After all, as you said, I'm the victim. My faith was threatened, and I took it out on Ashley, right?"

I tried to muster a commanding tone, but my words were barely audible. Frank just stared at me, shook his head, and covered the microphone.

"You disgust me. May Vexrus have mercy on your soul," he said while walking away, leaving me to face the entire nation alone.

Chapter 11

I leaned against the wall and slid to the floor. It was over. Regardless of how the trial ended, I would be banished to oblivion. Years of labor would easily kill me if a firing squad didn't. If Frank knew about the recordings, then Eleanor must have been telling the truth. I stared up at the ceiling, hoping that, as the last minutes of solitude I would experience in the world of the living passed, I would be sprung from my captors via divine intervention. I wondered what Vexrus thought of me; after all, I had only wanted to ensure that my friend's rights were respected. Had the State not forced my hand, Ashley would still be alive. If he had any concern for me, he chose not to make it known. I heard a knock at the conference room door followed by an order to come outside. My eyes darted around the room searching for a weapon miraculously placed there for me or some sign of divine mercy, but the door swinging open interrupted me. A pair of guards marched towards me as I sat quivering on the floor.

"It's time to go, Mr. Wilson," one of them said, and pulled me to my feet.

I nodded and stared at the floor as they marched me to the courtroom. Everyone in the spectator seats glared at me, as did the jury. Eleanor sat in the front row just behind the prosecution with a smug grin stretched across her face. The State determined and carried out Vexrus' will, and every institution of the State as well as its citizens despised me. In the elaborate wooden carvings on one of the walls, I saw our nation's flag wrapped around the Earth. Our nation was chosen by god, exalted over all others, but it was not Vexrus lording over all creation in this image; it was Visryan. A woman wearing a State media editor uniform clutched a copy of *The Book of Vexrus* as I passed. If high-level State employees, people who were supposedly ordained by god himself, despised me, that must have meant that god himself despised me as well.

In terms of functionality, god and the State were one in the same. I had even been a cog in the machine that made it so. If the State hated me, god hated me, and no amount of screaming, crying, or begging on the courtroom floor would change that. Citizens for whom the State and god had become separate were labeled heretics and eliminated, and Vexrus did nothing to stop it. Visryan often pointed to His lack of intervention as evidence that god was complicit in whatever it did. If the god I had been raised to worship existed, he wanted me to suffer. I was already damned, and perhaps because of that, I decided to bet on Reggie. I had been pushed into a corner from which there was no reasonable escape. My highest chance of survival was to hope for the unreasonable: that Vexrus did not exist.

The guards sat me down at a table next to the prosecutors. They were old, weathered, scholarly men, men who looked like they had spent the entirety of their lives in a dank basement pouring over case law. I had no lawyer, no access to research tools, and no warning that I would be forced into this impossible situation. This trial was deliberately unwinnable. Cameras captured my face at every angle. The promise of a legitimate trial may have been a lie from the start. From the moment I had been arrested, the prosecutors likely conspired to use me as a punching bag in front of the entire country.

"Would everyone please rise for Vexrus' Vicar and instrument of His will, Judge Arnold Johnson," a guard near the front of the room said.

Everyone stood as a small, hunchbacked man shuffled to the bench and took his seat. He wore a mantle depicting a battle between Vexrus' followers and those of some forgotten foreign power. Judges, who were legally considered to be vicars of god, wore these as a reminder of where their authority originates. There were many iterations of these, each featuring different art from Visryan's history. They often received them in elaborate ceremonies in which they knelt to Vexrus as the mantle was placed over them. On paper, they may have been called judges, but they were expected to remember who truly levied judgment in Visryan.

"Everyone but the jury may be seated. Bailiff, please swear the jury in," Judge Johnson said.

The guard who announced his entrance approached the jury, fished a piece of paper out of his pocket, and read aloud questions I had heard on countless courtroom dramas.

"Do you swear your unwavering loyalty to Vexrus and Visryan?" he asked.

"I do," they responded.

"Do you swear that you are committed to the advancement of Vexrus' State, as well as His people?"

"I do."

"Do you swear to render an honest verdict motivated by these commitments as well as the evidence presented here today?"

"I do."

"Thank you; you may be seated," Judge Johnson said, and directed the bailiff to return to his position.

The room fell silent. Judge Johnson adjusted his glasses and squinted at some notes in front of him.

"We will now commence with the trial of the Department of the Interior versus Marlow Wilson. Will the prosecution please levy their charges?"

"Gladly, Vicar. My name is Charles Hartford, and I'll be delivering the opening statement for the prosecution."

A tall man with a thin, bony face and receding hairline stood and addressed the jury, glancing at me out of the corner of his eye. I recognized this man. He had been cited as a case law expert on a couple of State-sponsored broadcasts. I believe he even worked with the Scholars in some capacity. The State spared no expense in arming my opponents.

"Ladies and gentlemen, what we have here is a clear case of heretical and violent behavior by a man who is undoubtedly damned. We have evidence of both heretical thought as well as lying to State officials from before, during, and after the heinous slaying of Ashley Davis. Today, we will not only prove that he routinely engages in this heretical thought throughout his daily life, but also that he is unrepentant man who deserves to be cast into oblivion," Charles said.

As he said those words, he looked over to me and smiled a little as if he was saying, "You can't stop me." He was lying about me. My record was absolutely spotless until I took Reggie's books, and they knew it. Did the desperation Eleanor witnessed at my apartment not suffice to prove that my faith was genuine? If the State was so certain of my guilt, why must they lie to prove it to the nation?

"He may try to persuade you with tales of his past service to the State or, we suspect, some nonsense narrative about how he suffered in the absence of his faith, but make no mistake, he has no interest in the preservation of Visryan. He only uses his government worker status as a shield against criticism. I assure you, this man does not embody the values of the State or the god that rules over it."

He scanned the room, looking first to the cameras, then to the spectators. He rested his gaze on the back left corner for a moment before returning to the jury. I extended my neck to see into the corner and found Frank. He had likely told the prosecution every detail of the defense we had prepared to prove his loyalty to the State. Before I even spoke, he had discredited my argument. A jury that had been primed to hate me for a week was already predisposed to ignore my arguments; now, it was all but guaranteed.

"The Department of the Interior will prove that he has engaged in a pattern of manipulative, anti-Visryan behavior including falsely swearing his belief, misrepresenting his intentions to State authorities, and circulating banned materials."

Charles turned toward the media crews in the back to address the remainder of the nation.

"Oftentimes in Visryan, I hear people say that the crime rate is so low that we don't even need the Department of the Interior."

Charles stood in front of my table and leaned forward as far as he could manage, his face nearly level with mine.

"Criminals like this prove that we do."

He spent another ten minutes or so assassinating my character, but I was too focused on formulating a response to listen. The argument Frank and I had developed was of no use. I would have to use Vexrus against the State. The prosecution as well as the system itself had spent the opening moments of the trial conflating the State and god as much as possible. In order to win, I had to separate them. Life as an employee of the State and an educated theocrat had given me the tools I needed. I knew how to convince others that god was on my side; in negotiations with foreigners, I was often tasked with doing so. Everything else Charles said about me was irrelevant. I would either put the State on trial, or I would soon be dead.

Charles concluded his statement and smiled at the jury as if to reassure them that they would soon be rid of the evil man he had just described.

"The prosecution rests, Vicar," he said while wiping some sweat from his brow.

"Thank you. You may be seated," Judge Johnson said, and turned to me.

"The defendant, Marlow Wilson, prisoner number nine-three-eight, may now deliver an opening statement in his defense or plead guilty to the charges as presented. Mr. Wilson, please stand and approach the bench."

I stood and walked toward him. Part of me expected to panic, but I was strangely calm. Either oblivion awaited me within minutes, or I would soon walk free. My crisis of faith had ended. There was no longer any need to lie about my past. I suddenly felt nothing for the god I had so faithfully served. My connection to the State had been effectively severed. I was free from all but death.

"Mr. Wilson, you may now either plead guilty to the charges of heresy, impersonating a State official, and murder, or argue for your innocence regarding one or more of these charges. How do you plead?"

I looked around the room. Every single person I saw believed me to be guilty. Political pundits had probably spent countless hours over the past week hypothesizing about what arguments the defense would make to avoid facing a firing squad.

"Not guilty," I replied in an even tone.

I turned around to see the bloodthirsty crowd and television cameras. I could see the confusion on the spectators' faces. Eleanor stared at me, mouth agape. People whispered to one another, and journalists frantically jotted down notes. Everyone had likely assumed that I would be begging for internment in a labor camp. Anyone who had watched media coverage of me would have thought that me proclaiming my innocence was laughable. A man near the front tried to covertly speak with the person next to him; he thought I was trying to commit suicide. Even Judge Johnson raised his eyebrows at my decision. After a long pause, he tapped his gavel and addressed the crowd.

"Order, order, please quiet down," he said, and the audience obeyed.

He looked down at me for a moment, and I up at him. Perhaps he was debating whether or not to ask if I wanted a moment to reconsider. I held his gaze for a few seconds, unwavering, eager to show my commitment. I wanted to tell him that dead men are fearless, that the moment god had abandoned me, I had become ungovernable.

"Very well, Mr. Wilson. You may now deliver your opening statement," he said and yielded the floor.

If my plan was to work, not only was it necessary for Vexrus to be a fiction of the State but I also had to present myself favorably to the audience. What I believed in that moment may have no longer mattered, but the audience's beliefs were of vital importance. For years I had made a living spreading Vexrus' word to clients overseas. I was a natural salesman. I looked at the Visryan insignia on the wall behind the judge and cleared my throat. Spectators leaned forward in their seats eager to hear the futile ravings of a suicidal mad man. I pointed at the top crown and addressed the crowd.

"Vexrus rules over all of us; does He not? Is He not the alpha and the omega? Is He not the arbiter of morality?" I inquired, eliciting confused mumbling from the onlookers.

A prosecutor raised his hand.

"Objection! In what way is this relevant to the charges? I for one don't want to hear a theological lecture from Marlow Wilson."

A few spectators laughed; even Judge Johnson struggled to suppress a giggle.

"I'll allow him to continue, assuming this is going somewhere. Continue, Mr. Wilson," Judge Johnson insisted.

"I assure you it is, Vicar," I said, narrowing my eyes at the prosecutors.

Judge Johnson nodded and motioned for me to continue.

"Testing Vexrus is both illegal as well as immoral. We are all well aware of this. Those who do so often meet with a terrible fate in this world and a worse one in the next, but now, in order to better serve my god and nation, I must break this rule. Vexrus has led me to this place so that I may expose those who seek to pervert His word and corrupt the minds of His people."

My tone grew gradually more commanding. I became increasingly confident as the prosecutors' faces reddened. Judge Johnson slammed his gavel down on the lectern with enough force to nearly crack it.

"Mr. Wilson, I will not have you promoting heretical behavior in this courtroom. This is not a house of sin! I demand that you cease doing so, or I will order the bailiff to kill you where you stand."

Veins bulged on his temples as he spoke. The bailiff's fingers traced his holster.

"If I am a heretic, why not let Vexrus save you the trouble? I plead not guilty, and if I am a liar, may Vexrus strike me down before you."

Many in the crowd gasped, including Eleanor. I braced myself for divine retribution. I was already destined for oblivion. Why not roll the dice and hope that Vexrus wasn't real? The prosecutors' eyes widened. Both the bailiff and Judge Johnson, not wanting to be engulfed in holy hellfire, left their positions, and moved toward the jury. Everyone in that room, myself included, expected for me to combust and die in agony, but nothing happened. The silence persisted for one minute, then another, then another. I had been spared. With a single utterance, god was dead, and in the eyes of millions of viewers around the nation, I was exonerated.

Judge Johnson shuffled back to his position and started to raise his gavel but did not tap it. He looked up at the Visryan insignia, then at me, unsure of how to proceed. I had broken the law, but in doing so, I had seemingly proven myself innocent via a grand gesture condoned by Vexrus. Before he could gather his thoughts, a juror stood up and cleared his throat, commanding the room's attention.

"Not guilty," he said.

Another juror did the same, followed by another. An official standing in the corner of the room quietly instructed the camera crews to cut the feed, but they ignored him. No one in that room had ever seen anyone test god directly, and none of them would dare to do so themselves. After all, their afterlives were guaranteed. They had far too much to lose. The remaining jurors gradually stood and delivered their verdicts in front of all of Visryan. It was unanimous. For the first time in my lifetime, a man tried for heresy pitted against the Department of the Interior had been cleared of all charges.

Chapter 12

The spectators talked amongst themselves, and the judge was too shocked to silence the room. I watched as Eleanor's expression turned from one of confusion to astonishment. One of the prosecutors began to hyperventilate. Another wrung his hands and shook his head while staring at the State seal. After whispering with his more-composed colleagues for a moment, one of the prosecutors stood and addressed the court.

"People, people, calm down. Now, I don't know what that was exactly, but Visryan has laws that are to be followed. If you see the evidence we have collected, you'll find that, without a shadow of a doubt, Mr. Wilson is guilty as charged," he said, his voice cracking a little.

"What you have is fiction cooked up by corrupt bureaucrats who no longer serve their god," I said.

The crowd once again fell silent. People who wanted my head ten minutes earlier now no longer knew who to believe. I felt a strange surge of power. For the first time in my life, I was in no way beholden to the State, and as I looked at the shocked expressions around me, I realized that, perhaps, the State was beholden to me.

"That's insanity. Right here, we have pictures of---"

"I know what you have. The fact is that the upper echelon of the Visryan government wanted to suppress truthful information about Vexrus. I had books with new, inarguable proofs of god's existence, one's that would have altered our understanding of the divine, but instead of embracing this wonderful truth, they hunted me like an animal. That sacred knowledge may be lost forever because of people like you! But look, Vexrus had guided me to this place so that I can expose this evil! Every step of the way, He held my hand and whispered in my ear what to say to each of you in order to stand before you now."

I kept my story vague. I feared antagonizing the wrong group of people. If I gestured at nebulous, systemic corruption, everyone could claim to be against it, and more importantly, no one would be able to debunk it. The official in the corner of the room once again ordered the camera crews to cut the feed, but they refused. They would not dare defy god's will. Vexrus wanted the nation to hear my words, and no paper-shuffling bureaucrat would interfere. Charles stood and marched toward me.

"I can't stand to hear any more of this. You lied to the State on multiple occasions, and murdered a good citizen. Now you flaunt your heresy in front of the nation. Children could be watching this garbage! Judge Johnson, I call for the revocation of his right to defend himself in court on the grounds that allowing him to do so is a detriment to the nation."

He looked up at Judge Johnson, who ran his fingers across the worn handle of his gavel.

"To do so may be in violation of my oath. I swore to serve Vexrus first and the State second. If those two bodies ever conflict, I know which side I'm on," he said to Charles' horror.

Despite the horde of State-loyal police around me, I felt bulletproof.

"He's right. Visryan, as it sits, cannot properly serve Vexrus. It needs to be reoriented to serving god rather that its elites, but of course, you all know that, don't you?" I asked with an air of superiority.

Obviously, these men had no idea what I was talking about, but they did not have to. The people watching me simply had to believe that some group of people had conspired against Vexrus and, by extension, me.

"How dare you! I have served the State faithfully for my entire life! Look at what I've done. The filth I've purged from society," Charles responded.

"What was it you said earlier? 'He only uses his government worker status as a shield against criticism?' The projection is palpable," I said.

Charles turned to the jury, surprised to see them scowling at him.

"Can't you people see that he's lying to you? Allow me to show you the evidence against him before you reach a verdict."

The evidence he had could potentially harm my newfound credibility in the eyes of the public, so I thought it wise to strike preemptively. Eleanor seemed receptive to my message; after all, she was remarkably zealous in her belief. The Vexrus she knew would not have allowed me to challenge Him without good reason. She repeatedly glanced at the pistol on her hip. I did not know who she considered shooting, but perhaps I could influence her decision.

"Eleanor Riley, I know that you were not privy to their plan. Vexrus will spare you. You were a tool of those ranked above you. Redeem yourself now and kill these corrupt prosecutors," I said.

Vexrus was not real. Some State official other than I must have known. The person who ordered the cameras to be shut off perhaps. The Department of the Interior likely housed some of those who were aware of the true nature of Visryan, but I did not believe Eleanor to be among them. Her behavior was too zealous to not be borne of genuine faith. From her belief in my love of the State to the disappointment in her face when I betrayed her trust, she seemed far too genuine to be complicit in the gaslighting of a nation. She wanted to serve her god however she could, and I was more than happy to give her that opportunity.

The bailiff pointed his gun at my head and someone in the crowd screamed. His finger grazed the trigger, but he chose not to kill me. It was his duty to protect the people in the courtroom, but it was also his duty to serve his deity, which, for all intents and purposes, was me.

"I've heard the recordings, Marlow," Eleanor said, her voice wavering She stared at the State seal, shoulders slumped, perhaps unsure of her place in a world where the State was fallible.

"I said what I had to; Vexrus guided my words. If it weren't His will, I would never have said or done the things I did, and I am willing to invoke god's wrath to prove it. Can they say the same?" I said and pointed at the prosecutors.

The bailiff slowly lowered his weapon, and everyone watched the prosecutors. My trial had ended, but theirs had just begun.

"Well, can you?" asked Eleanor.

Charles' lips quivered. Could he have known the truth, as well? He may have been contemplating the possibility of Vexrus' non-existence in that moment. If he were to make the same claim as I had, I would no longer have a monopoly on divinity. They all had to die before they got that chance.

"Kill them, now," I reiterated.

Charles backed away from me and slid down in a chair behind the prosecutor's table. He scowled at me. He may have wanted to test god, to tread where I had, but if he were wrong in doing so, he would lose everything, and he knew it. The oldest prosecutor stood, rested his hands on the table, and squeezed his eyes shut in anticipation of a bullet. The others remained silent, presumably confused as to why their god had abandoned them. Eleanor scanned the room. The cameras were all centered on her. She could serve Vexrus or the State, not both.

"His will be done," Eleanor said and pointed her gun at them.

She fired a round into each of their heads on national television. None of them ran or fought or protested. Perhaps they thought that they had been abandoned, or were merely cogs in the cosmic machine. She killed the one that stood first, followed by the others in a line. When the first one's corpse fell to the ground, the others began to cry. Charles was the last to die. He gritted his teeth and clenched his fists. He suppressed his instinctual urge to survive in favor of obedience to the State's teachings. I knew he wanted to lash out at me, to call me a fraud and a liar, but he simply could not take the risk. He spent his last moments fighting the natural human desire to stay alive. His brief defiance may have set him apart from the others, but his corpse crumpled and fell like the rest.

An eerie silence fell over the courtroom as they lay still on the floor. The gnawing guilt I felt looking at images of Ashley began to manifest again. These men were tools of liars in the highest echelons of government. They suffered under the same delusion I once had. Charles was my opposition, but he acted in what he thought to be Visryan's best interest. Now he was dead. Was the guilt mine to shoulder? What choice did I have? The State and the myth of Vexrus forced my hand. His survival jeopardized my own, and, given death's new permanence, I decided that was justification enough.

"Well done, Eleanor. The State is rife with corruption, and Vexrus has brought me to purge it. I will see to it that not only does every good citizen enter the afterlife but also that those who try to muzzle our deity are purged."

She was shaking. Those prosecutors had served the Department of the Interior; she and they had probably been well acquainted. If she was willing to kill her colleagues for a man whom she claimed to despise, surely her faith was legitimate. None of the guards intervened. When I entered, I was a dead man going through the motions of waiting for my inevitable guilty verdict. Now, I was the judge and jury, and anyone who supported me was a potential executioner. Eleanor walked up to me, put her arm across her chest, and took a knee, the characteristic bow of the Department of the Interior.

"I'm sorry, Marlow. For my entire life, I had considered myself to be a good citizen working to ensure that everyone can enter the afterlife. I can't believe I---"

I put my hand on her shoulder. She looked up at me, teary eyed. As I took one last look at the people I had slain,

I felt a sudden urge to tell her I was a fraud, that the State lied, that Vexrus was fiction, but the armed guards questioning their loyalty outside prevented me from doing so. I was a coward, but had anyone else been in such a predicament, they would have kept their mouth shut, as well.

"It's okay. There was no way you could've known. Citizens like you keep Visryan running. Both I and Vexrus are proud of your devotion."

She smiled and breathed a sigh of relief. She must have thought of herself as a traitor to her god. The tears streaming down her face conveyed that I had freed her from a stomach-turning dread, perhaps the same one from which she had once freed me.

"I will execute any orders you give me. As far as I'm concerned, your word outweighs the Department of the Interior or even the Supreme Council, and I know several others who would agree with me after seeing this," Eleanor explained calmly.

"You're a good citizen, Eleanor."

Both the State officials as well as the citizens in the courtroom echoed the same sentiment. Regardless of what they had been taught, they saw Vexrus defend a mere mortal from the once-infallible State. Their theology had been irrevocably altered. The State had shown the people how to enact god's will since the country's founding, but they were suddenly unfit to do so. The people needed someone who Vexrus trusted to guide them.

There was no legal precedent for this, and no one would dare raise a hand to me after what they had witnessed. I turned to the bailiff and pointed at my shackled legs. He looked to Judge Johnson, who shrugged.

"Well, take them off," Eleanor said, glaring at the pair.

"I'm not really sure if I'm supposed to do that, ma'am," the bailiff answered.

"As we've all just seen, Marlow Wilson is an innocent man. It's your duty to free him. Unless of course, you still think he's guilty," she said.

The bailiff scratched his chin and ran his fingers over the key.

"So be it," he said.

He knelt down and undid my shackles under Eleanor's close supervision. The other armed guards in the room held their hands up and backed away from me. The official who had attempted to cut the camera feed tapped his fingers against his holster. I motioned for Eleanor to lend me her ear.

"Hey, do you think you can get us to somewhere safe?" I whispered.

She caught sight of the official and scanned the rest of the room. Before answering, she positioned herself between him and me.

"Yeah, I have a massive list of isolated properties," she said. "I'm going to call some of my co-workers and see if they can transport us."

The bailiff took the shackles off and retreated to the bench. It seemed that I was indeed free to leave.

"Will they really do that?" I asked.

"If they saw what I did, they will," Eleanor replied.

She escorted me out of the courtroom with her pistol drawn, though it seemed that these people were no longer a threat. Once we were alone running through the courthouse, she called some of her subordinates and arranged transport for us. I could not discern what they said, but their tones were frantic.

"They'll pick us up in front of the courthouse soon. We need to hurry," she said.

We saw hordes of viewers gathered on the courtroom steps through the glass double doors. They looked neither violent nor distraught. They just stared at their phones in disbelief. Eleanor's phone buzzed, telling her that her subordinates would soon arrive. Journalists crowded the courthouse door as Eleanor slowly slid it open. They begged for an explanation for what I had done, but the risk of a would-be assassin being among them prevented me from engaging with them, not that I would have known what to say. Eleanor stepped out before me and fired a round into the air.

"Back up! If you come near either of us, I'll kill you on the spot!" she shouted.

The horde split and retreated to either side of the stairs. I descended the stairs in a flurry of camera flashes. Some of the people reached out to touch me or begged me for some sort of blessing. Fanatical hatred had been replaced by fanatical adoration in a matter of minutes. The cardboard signs they had used to taunt me on my ride to the courthouse now lay abandoned in the street. Five black cars with tinted windows and a white van pulled up to the curb. A dozen or so Department of the Interior agents flooded out and pointed guns at the crowd. A few warning shots rang out followed by an order to stand still. I had expected to ride away from the courthouse in one of their vehicles, but as a prisoner, not as their ally. One of them held a door open for me. As it closed, I caught a glimpse of the Visryan flag blowing in the wind. I had indeed become a king through Vexrus.

The driver craned his neck to look back at me.

"It's an honor to meet you, Mr. Wilson. You'll be safely hidden within the hour," he said. "We've got shelter, security, and even some of your clothes from the evidence locker."

Eleanor got in the seat beside me.

"Go before the State can start tailing us," she said.

The caravan pulled away from the courthouse and onto the expressway. We soon scattered and became untraceable. I could have been in any one of the countless Department of the Interior cars spread across the city. The State had larger issues to tackle, however; they had been denounced by their god on national television.

Chapter 13

My trial occupied every news station for days, and support for all State institutions plummeted. Citizens that had once followed any order given by the State without question now protested in front of Vexrus study institutes. Fundraising institutions that had once benefited the State ceased to do so, and sought better ways to serve their god. Soldiers deserted at ever-increasing rates. For centuries, god and the State had been one in the same. No one had seen any meaningful distinction between the two. Now, the State and god were at odds with one another, and as any Visryan would tell you, Vexrus could offer more than the fallible humans in government ever could.

Officially, the State was still hunting me a week later, but the populace seemed uninterested in assisting it. Eleanor and dozens of her colleagues had deserted and brought me to a secluded cabin tucked behind a grove of trees on the edge of Relis. It was a dreary little thing—termite-ridden wood and an old wood-burning stove for heating. The central room was littered with cots for my new subordinates. Every part of the building creaked at the slightest breeze. Headlights would occasionally penetrate the leafless trees and stretch across the ceiling of my bedroom. I would wonder if it were a squad of loyalist hitmen who had somehow gotten my location. A cracking branch or animal shuffling around in the dark would keep me awake for hours. It reminded me of my brief internment at the jail, fearing the faintest bump in the night. After all, the room was no larger than my jail cell had been, and I was not free to travel outside of the building.

Eleanor and her colleagues were security experts. The Department of the Interior often housed important witnesses in undisclosed remote locations and kept watch over them. This skillset translated well. A minimum of five of them stayed scattered around the property at any given moment. At least one was required to stay outside and another inside. I forbade them from monitoring me in my tiny bedroom; I needed somewhere where I wasn't god's elect. They mostly sat around in the living room, peering out of the windows looking for threats and waiting for me to bestow some sort of manifesto from heaven upon them. I kept delaying them, imploring them to be patient while I hovered over a small television in my room and scoured media networks hoping that an answer would present itself. My followers had faith that I would eventually commune with Vexrus and be given a plan to rescue the State from the nebulous enemies I had conjured.

Devin Phillips, one of the guards who had escorted me to the prisoner transport after I killed Ashley, constantly requested to be on my security detail. He was an overweight man with a cheerful disposition who towered over everyone around him. Often when I was sitting on the corner of my tiny twin bed looking out of the window, I would see him out of the corner of my eye standing on the porch outside staring at me with a hopeful, expectant look on his face. Those around me were certain of my ability. After all, Devin believed Vexrus chose me to share His message. I was the only person in the nation who was aware that a criminal had lucked into a mythic position in the minds of the masses.

In the midst of faking a divine prerogative, I had to contend with the possibility of my own mortality once again. The agony I experienced when I first read Reggie's books crept out from the recesses of my mind and often interfered with my planning. I felt oblivion lapping at my feet, but my immediate survival had to take precedent. None of those around me knew that I had covertly disproven their god's existence. If I were to tell them, the consequences could be dire. My only option was to bury my misery until a later date. Avoiding oblivion was still as powerful a motivator as it had been when I was faithful. I had no choice but to press onward, and Vexrus was the perfect tool for doing so. Only when Vexrus became fiction did He truly begin to benefit me.

I spent much of my time alone in my bedroom scouring news networks to gauge the country's reaction to what I had done. The media companies that had once delivered essentially identical news that supported the State now began to differ from one another. Visryan's hold over the institutions that controlled the flow of information was weakening, and as it did so, more of my supporters were able to voice their opinions. The old guard, State-aligned media barely acknowledged my existence, but privately operated outlets and some rebellious local stations started changing the narrative. It seemed that my trial had galvanized faithful citizens across the nation.

My supporters were diffuse but numerous, and the State seemed to fear them. They called themselves the Vexrus First movement, after what Judge Johnson had said at the trial. His claim that he served "Vexrus first and the State second" seemed to resonate with the newly disaffected masses. They all proclaimed my innocence and expressed a disdain for the apparently corrupt State. There was no leadership structure, only loosely organized groups of disillusioned angry theocrats seemingly deprived of their theocracy. Even in my absence, they looked to me for guidance. After what they saw at the trial, I was the only religious authority left. I was confident that if I were to speak to these people, they would listen to me.

Perhaps I, inspired by a vision from the divine, could dismantle some of the State's barbaric institutions. But would whoever knew the truth allow me to do so? What about the faithful? Would they tolerate radical changes without questioning their dogma? My behavior needed to match what was expected of Vexrus. I could not risk accidentally dispelling the illusion. I had been pushed into a corner and reacted in the only way I could. Another distraught citizen could not be permitted to do the same.

Before trying to influence people en masse, however, I thought it wise to remove the skeletons from my closet. The prosecutors from the trial had already been eliminated, but there was at least one other person who had heard the recordings and had intimate knowledge of my crimes: Franklin. He could not be allowed to contact any journalists or authorities.

Despite being a deserter, Eleanor still had access to The Department of the Interior's database of every Relis citizen's personal information, including their addresses. According to Eleanor, my newfound influence had spread throughout the Department of the Interior to such a degree that the organization could no longer function. Even within the largely State-loyal Relis headquarters, I had allies willing to risk their lives to ensure our success. If I were to catch Franklin, it needed to be before I made any public proclamations, lest he go into hiding.

Eleanor arrived for her turn on security detail on a crisp morning nine days after my trial. Her eyes looked sunken in. Staying ahead of the authorities had been an exhausting job, and I did little to illustrate my value since she brought me there.

"Eleanor, I need your help with something."

Her face lit up when I spoke, and she rushed to my side.

"Yes? What is it?" she asked eagerly.

"Franklin Bradford, my almost-lawyer, was instrumental in that fraudulent trial. I think it would be best for the nation if problematic elements such as he were to be eliminated. After all, there isn't any room for dishonest people like him in a functioning theocracy," I said, trying to muster the commanding tone I had utilized at the trial.

"Why do you want me to kill Franklin? Aren't there more high priority targets to go after? He has basically nothing to do with the Visryan government," she asked, perplexed.

I had to explain how it was in the people's best interest that Franklin be eliminated. Of course, it wasn't. He was of no consequence to any State endeavor, but he could potentially call my new position of power into question. I held no legitimate office. I avoided a large-scale manhunt solely because the people held me in such high regard and their faith in the State was all but gone. If the citizenry were to turn against me, I would once again find myself in a jail cell, or worse. Fortunately, as Vexrus' apparent messenger, I had a bottomless supply of justification.

"I worry that he may expose those recordings to media outlets or the Supreme Council. If an already confused, distraught citizen was to hear them, they may become erratic,"

I explained. "Besides, he helped to orchestrate that witch hunt. Vexrus would rather such a heretic not remain in His nation."

"Well, if that's what He wants, consider it done," she said sternly.

If she felt conflicted, she did not make it known. She simply nodded, fished a cell phone out of her pocket, and began coordinating the attack. She seemed pleased to have an order to follow. Within ten minutes, she was tracking his location through his phone.

In under a minute, I had ordered a man be killed, and the Department of the Interior was going to carry that order out. In exchange for shouldering the horrid truth, I had been granted more power than a faithful citizen could have ever imagined. I watched as Eleanor talked with her subordinates. It took so little for me to set this attack in motion. Even though I considered Frank to be my enemy, I detested orchestrating such violence. I told myself that, once the immediate threats to my safety were dealt with, I would atone by improving the nation.

My followers distributed weapons among themselves and started for the door with a sense of urgency. Eleanor approached me and showed me a roadmap on her phone.

"He's driving on the expressway in our direction. In about fifteen minutes, I suspect that he'll get off exit eleven to go to his house. We can set up a barricade at that exit and capture him immediately, if you're okay with it."

It crossed my mind that he could attempt to convert my supporters by delivering arguments the prosecutors would have used. Even in custody, he was a threat.

"You don't need to capture him, only kill him. Vexrus has already given you the go-ahead. A trial would be a waste of time and resources. He has already been found guilty."

Eleanor hesitated for a moment, then nodded. She seemed to care little for how Visryan law regarded her actions. My opinion, and Vexrus', was of far greater importance.

"Oh, do you think I could come along?" I asked Eleanor. "I've been cooped up in here for over a week."

"I'm not sure it would be safe," she replied. Someone from the Scholar-loyal sects of the Department of the Interior could see you."

It was vital that I confirm her and the others' loyalty. So much time had passed since the trial that I feared their fanatical devotion had weakened. I needed to see if they were truly willing to kill for me.

"I'll stay in the car. Besides, Vexrus won't allow harm to come to me. He already protected me once," I insisted.

She sighed and relented. She, Devin, and I piled into a stolen Department of the Interior vehicle, and four others along with traffic barricades rode in a van. We drove down the expressway mostly in silence. From the security of my cabin, I had not seen the profound effect my trial had had locally. Shattered windows covered the sidewalks in front of

State-owned buildings. Graffiti claiming that State officials were false prophets coated overpasses and alleyways. There were no repairmen or police officers. The city had evidently been left to rot.

"Where are the police?" I asked.

"Most of them quit. They didn't want to serve the State anymore," Devin said. "Actually, most government employees don't."

"A lot of people don't see a point in toiling away at their jobs if afterlife credit has no value," Eleanor chimed in. "Aside from a skeleton staff, most State buildings are empty."

The afterlife credit system motivated society, and I had destroyed it. If I were going to align the people with me, I had to give them their chance at entering heaven back. Years negotiating for cheaper goods for the State had taught me the value of quantifying one's afterlife status. Whoever holds the key to eternity controls the masses. I would not be considered a hero for long if my heroism only resulted in the destruction of Visryan's infrastructure and social services. Screeching breaks pulled me from my thoughts.

"We're here," Devin said.

Everyone except for me exited the vehicles and began setting up a roadblock. Night had almost fallen. Frank would not be able to see the roadblock until he was too close to turn back. The van group hid in a ditch about thirty yards from the barricade while the others stood near it. Eleanor monitored his location on her phone. One member of the van group, a short man with thick glasses named Arnold, inspected an automatic rifle while he waited. Eleanor put her phone away and retreated behind the barricade, followed by the others. Shortly after, a car pulled off of the expressway and approached. It neared the roadblock and stopped. A moment later, the van's headlights turned on and illuminated the vehicle. Inside sat Frank.

"Sir, please turn off your vehicle" one of them said through a megaphone.

Frank obeyed and shut it off. Devin and two others stepped into the road and approached his window. They tried to appear non-threatening. Devin waved and knocked on Frank's window as the others meandered around behind him.

"Please let your window down, sir," Devin said.

Franklin cracked it and looked up at him.

"This is just a routine search for contraband. Would you please exit the vehicle? We'll be done in a few minutes and get you on your way."

After he spoke, Frank's expression turned to one of horror. He frantically juggled his keys around before putting them in his ignition and cranking the engine. Perhaps he caught a glimpse of Eleanor or me, and panicked.

"Sir, shut your vehicle off now!" he shouted.

Arnold emerged from the ditch and took aim at the car. Frank shifted into reverse and mashed the gas pedal. He barely dodged Frank's car as it hurdled backwards. Eleanor shouted something, and one of her colleagues drove the van into the street, blocking Frank. In an attempt to dodge the van, Frank turned sharply and slid into the ditch on the opposite side of the road with a screech. I exited the car and walked over to the ditch as my subordinates surrounded Frank. His horn blared, and the slight scent of burnt rubber wafted up from the road. Lying face down on an airbag was Frank.

"Marlow, get back in the car!" Eleanor demanded, but I ignored her.

Frank looked up, a stream of blood running down his face. I stepped in front of his headlights so that he could see me clearly. I wanted him to know that he had not betrayed me without consequence. He likely knew that I was after him when he saw Eleanor step into view, but I wanted there to be no cause for doubt. His collusion with my enemies would not go unpunished. This was a necessary measure. How would exposing my lie benefit the State? It needed a leader, and Frank stood in the way of that. He scowled at me as Arnold approached him. Frank fished around in his center console as he took aim. A shiny piece of metal caught the light from the van's headlights.

Frank bolted out of his car and started in my direction. I then realized that he was holding a gun. Evidently, Frank still had faith in the State and was willing to die to prevent me from subverting it further.

"You've ruined my country!" he shouted as he ran into the street.

Eleanor jumped in front of me and pulled her pistol from its holster, but before he could take aim, Arnold fired. A dozen or so rounds tore through him and his weapon fell to the asphalt with a clink. He staggered forward before falling to one knee, then on his face. I wondered if he felt like Reggie. He knew the truth but was powerless to enlighten anyone, and the very nature of what he knew made him a target. He fought against and within a machine that was more complex than he could ever understand and, ultimately, it killed him. Eleanor remained in front of me while Arnold walked over to Frank and planted a round in the back of his head.

"I told you to stay in the car," Eleanor said with a concerned tone.

"Lesson learned," I responded.

They were unquestionably loyal. They were willing to die to protect me. These deserters did not require my oversight, and if my other supporters were half as loyal, they would not either. Faith moderated their behavior as it once had mine. With their help, I could tie up the remaining loose ends and begin legitimizing my power in both the eyes of the faithful and secret skeptics alike.

One question remained, however. If these former agents of the Department of the Interior were so zealous, who was aware of Vexrus' non-existence? The man who ordered the camera crews to cut the feed at my trial seemed unmoved by my demonstration. Perhaps some factions within the organization knew of and suppressed the true nature of reality. Then I thought of the group most intimately involved with the production of *The Book of Vexrus*: the Scholars. The deity described within the book was undoubtedly fictitious, and the authors must have known it. They lived longer than everyone else primarily because they, as a general rule, never committed suicide to enter paradise sooner. Why would they do this if they believed in Vexrus? The fear of god had no power over a non-believer, but the fear of oblivion certainly did. They had also been suspiciously quiet since the trial. Considering that they were presumably the highest theocratic authorities on the face of the Earth, it seemed strange that they were not eager to comment on what I had done or offer an explanation as to why Vexrus had let a guilty man challenge Him on national television. Their most loyal adherents resented me. If I became the highest theocratic authority, I would supplant their position.

I thought of Albert Woodward, the Scholar with whom I had spoken during my crisis of faith. Vexrus was not real, and he knew it. He had sat across from me and lied to my face. If I were going to survive to old age, I had to consolidate power before the legitimacy of my stunt at the trial was called into question. I needed to be the only person who knew the truth. Anyone else was a liability. I told everyone that I would purge Visryan of the unfaithful, and, aside from myself, I intended to deliver on that promise.

Chapter 14

State officials deserted their positions at ever-increasing rates during the next few days. Many of them joined civilian groups that were dedicated to my service. Political pundits debated what I had done to the country on every news outlet. Disillusioned citizens gathered at monuments and population centers and begged me to tell them what to do en masse. They had no guidance and needed it desperately. Despite me having no way to contact the masses, they expected direction as they were accustomed to frequent divine instruction. The Vexrus First movement, which was gradually solidifying into a legitimate force from masses of splintered cells, realized this, as well.

"Marlow, can I come in?" Devin said and knocked on my door.

I sat up and rubbed my eyes. The clock on the wall read 5:45 a.m. I ran over to the window and peaked outside through a hole in the curtains. Outside was still, dark, and quiet. I stretched and fished around in the dark for some clothes.

"Give me a second."

I yawned and opened the door to see an ecstatic Devin.

"What's going on? Is there a problem?" I inquired.

He handed me a cell phone.

"We have lines of communication with multiple Vexrus First groups that spawned out of the fractured Department of the Interior, and we'll probably get more soon. We've been vetting this information for the past couple of hours."

I looked it over. On the screen was contact information for various Vexrus First organizations arranged alphabetically by location. There were nearly twenty of them. I turned the phone over in my hand searching for abnormalities.

"No one is tracking it. I assure you this is as secure as it gets," he said. "That's our area of expertise, after all."

"I'm honestly surprised that so much of the Department of the Interior turned on Visryan so readily," I replied. "Not that I'm ungrateful."

"Well, the way I see it, we are unquestionably loyal to Vexrus. If that means betraying the State, so be it. I guess they agree."

His explanation made sense. Intellectually, I agreed with him, but my tenuous grip on power and the ease with which one could have taken it from me led me to search for traitors regardless.

"Let's hope so. I'll speak with each one individually, then set up a conference call."

Devin crossed his arms over his chest and smiled a childish smile. These people, my followers, were shockingly carefree given that we were essentially plotting a coup. Whether they lived or died, paradise awaited. Why would the moral implications of toppling Visryan's institutions concern them? I was the only person who would have to live with the decisions I made. No matter what they were ordered to do, their hands were tied. They were merely tools of an entity beyond their comprehension.

I spoke with the leadership of each of these groups, and found only complete devotion. Deserter factions existed within every major district from the port city of Helias to Alexandria, the capital. Other groups outside of the ones I could contact existed, those composed of regular citizens, but I needed professionalism, not a militia of vigilantes. They all seemed willing to consolidate under the Vexrus First movement, but required specific targets. The enemy I had concocted was deliberately shapeless, but it could not remain so forever, there had to actually be something hiding in the dark.

During my conversation with the group based in the capital, I decided to raise the subject of eliminating the Scholars. They were regarded highly by the State and the populace alike. I worried that lashing out at them would disqualify me as god's speaker outright. In an earlier meeting, the Alexandria sect had stricken me as particularly eager to act. I thought the woman with whom I had spoken then to be a suitable subject to test the waters.

"What if the people Vexrus marks for dead are theocratic authorities? Would you still be prepared to act?" I asked.

She went silent, inhaled, and exhaled. She had been talkative until that point. My divinely ordained position clashed with theirs. Most of these groups likely expected me to target government bureaucrats or someone in the private sector, but not those who maintained the sacred book.

"If it's what He asks of me, consider it done," she said.

I decided to press her. There could be no hesitation. If I were to order an attack on the Scholars, I needed to be certain that it would be carried out.

"You hesitated for a moment. Are you sure you're willing? If you aren't, we can put someone else in charge. I don't blame you; it takes a lot of devotion to commit to something like this."

I heard a faint gasp on the other end of the line. Hopefully, I had offended her.

"I am willing. I promise. It's just a shock to think that people in such a position could be plotting against Vexrus."

I went silent for a moment. I wanted the members of the Vexrus First movement to beg me to give them orders. I was not going to justify myself to her; she was going to justify herself to me.

"I really am loyal to the cause. I was just caught off guard; that's all," she pleaded. The desperation in her voice was palpable.

"Well alright, that's what I like to hear," I finally said. "There'll be a conference call between the leadership of various Vexrus First groups around eleven o'clock tonight. I expect you to be there."

"Yes sir, of course. I wouldn't miss it."

Before I could proceed with my attack order, however, I needed more information about the Scholars from the source. Fortunately, I could accomplish this and rid my closet of another skeleton simultaneously by capturing and killing Albert Woodward. But placing him in Eleanor's custody could have endangered me. Operating under the assumption that he knew of Vexrus' non-existence, he could claim that he was god's elect and potentially turn my own forces against me. He was likely aware of this. I could not discern why he or another Scholar had not employed this tactic already. The threat of imminent death, however, may have forced his hand. As long as I prevented him from uttering anything problematic, I would be safe. The idea of capturing him myself crossed my mind, but if I neared his office, State officials would shoot me on sight. The night before, I had Eleanor gather data about him. I knew where he lived, worked, and spent his free time. I also knew what he drove. I decided to write him a letter and have one of my subordinates leave it on his windshield. It would warn him that, if he opened his mouth, he would be killed immediately. Hopefully, that could stall him until he was gagged. I would then have him escorted to the cabin where I could interrogate him one on one.

Initially, the contingent of ten Vexrus Firsters I had chosen to carry out the order expressed confusion at my requirements. Eleanor recommended catching him as he exited his car at his home after work, but I stressed the importance of him seeing my letter first.

"Why does it matter when he sees it? We can make him read it on the way back," One of the younger Vexrus Firsters said.

My subordinates sat on the corners of their cots struggling to hear me over the cacophony of rain on the cabin's tin roof. I needed to ensure that they would prioritize Albert seeing it while also not being tempted to read it themselves.

"I'm not at liberty to tell you. That message is from Vexrus, for Woodward's eyes only. Let him take the letter, read it, then when he looks up, be standing in front of him with your weapons drawn. Afterwards, take the letter and, without reading it, burn it," I said.

"Do we really need to kill him if he talks? That seems a bit harsh. What if he is just reacting to us approaching him?" an older Vexrus Firster asked.

"I guarantee that he will understand the situation *after* he reads it. Also, you aren't waiting for him to talk. If he so

165

much as parts his lips, you are to put a bullet in his head. Is that clear?" I asked.

Everyone nodded in agreement but exchanged looks of concern.

"The security risks are just too much to ignore. The State may have lost some of its influence, but the Institute of Vexrus Studies will still be heavily guarded," Devin said.

"Have some faith. I assure you that everything will work out for the best. He gets off work at six, and I need to speak with him before the conference call with the heads of the other Vexrus First groups tonight. Get him back here quickly. Everyone is dismissed to begin preparations."

They all stood and started for the door. After the majority of them had filed out, I asked Eleanor and Devin to stay behind for a moment.

"Eleanor, I need you to stay here. Some of the other groups' leadership may call and want to discuss strategy, and I told them you would be available."

"You want me to stay here? That leaves the others without a leader."

"No, it won't. I'm putting Devin in charge. He's been your subordinate for a long time, right? Surely, he's qualified to capture an old man."

Eleanor hesitated, but understood that my, or at least Vexrus', authority trumped hers.

"Well, alright. Good luck, Devin."

She looked dejected. I hated to damage her ego. Devin was ecstatic, though he shouldn't have been. I knew exactly how dangerous kidnapping a Scholar in the parking lot of a State institution would be. There would likely be casualties, and I could not afford to lose someone as competent as Eleanor. Devin was the most trustworthy person I was willing to lose. In the case that they were attacked, I could trust Devin to kill Albert before dying himself. I sent Eleanor away and spoke with Devin alone.

"I need you to feed me audio of the kidnapping. If Albert says anything, I need to hear it, and you need to kill him."

Devin nodded, but appeared confused.

"What are you worried that he'll say?"

I thrust a lavalier microphone into his hands, looking around for eavesdroppers.

"I can't tell you. Just make sure he stays quiet. Ensure that the letter is burned, as well. A lot is riding on you."

"I'll do whatever you ask of me, or at least try my best," Devin told me.

I placed my hand on his shoulder. I was grateful to have supporters that were so willing to die to carry out an order.

"I know. I believe in you, Devin, and Vexrus does, as well."

He beamed with satisfaction.

The hours ticked by, and my supporters prepared their equipment. Eleanor micromanaged the preparations. She was obviously worried for their safety, but was too faithful to question my decision. Part of me worried that, if we suffered too many casualties, she may lose faith in me as a leader, but Vexrus would hopefully be there to justify any unforeseen losses.

At 5:30 that night, nine of my supporters, led by Devin, departed. Only Devin and I knew about the audio feed. It was true that I wanted to hear anything Albert might have said, but I also wanted to spy on my supporters. I wanted constant reassurance of their devotion so that I could cut off any rot before it spread to the others.

Based on the conversations I overheard, they arrived around 5:50 and immediately placed the letter on his windshield. Fortunately, their Department of the Interior uniforms added an aesthetic of legitimacy to their activities. Devin remarked that any citizens who looked over at them did so with only disdain for the State they had once worshipped, not suspicion. About fifteen minutes later, one of them said that they saw Albert staggering to his car, cane in hand. About two minutes of silence passed before I heard one of them say, "He's reading it. Go." Multiple doors groaned open, and boots hit the pavement. I heard some indiscernible yelling, but it did not sound like Albert. I hoped that he understood his situation. Devin, who I hypothesize was placing duct tape over Albert's mouth, handed the letter to a subordinate named Cynthia and ordered her to burn it. Seconds later, they started sprinting. I think one of them yelled, "Start the goddamned van!" I then heard the familiar crack of gunshots. They had been caught in the act. I could discern little from the symphony of gunfire and corpses hitting the pavement. Eventually, I heard one of the van doors open and a groaning Devin climb inside. Rounds puncturing metal and shattered glass scattering across the floor obscured their speech as they sped away. The details eluded me, but I knew for certain that we had sustained heavy damage. A few seconds later, the audio cut completely.

I returned to my bedroom and watched the tattered curtains sway softly back and forth. As Visryan descended further into chaos and my future grew progressively more uncertain, I had become colder. When I felt oblivion encircle me, the people around me became resources to prolong my life and cement my power, but when that fear subsided, I was left with the guilt of what I had done. It was a vicious cycle. I resolved to persevere through the carnage, telling myself that the good I would do as Visryan's leader would outweigh the things I had done to attain the position.

Eleanor sat on the front porch staring off into the night, desperate to see the van's headlights approach. I sat next to her and put my hand on her shoulder. I wanted to tell her that I thought they would be fine, but I knew that we had suffered losses to some degree. I could not offer disingenuous reassurances without jeopardizing my perceived infallibility, so I just sat with her in silence. I had nearly given them up for dead when our bullet-riddled, blood-soaked van rolled into view. They stopped in front of the cabin and tossed a battered Albert Woodward out of the back door and onto the ground. Eleanor ran up to them eager to offer medical care. Of the nine that left an hour or two earlier, four remained. Devin, who had been shot in the abdomen, Cynthia, who escaped unharmed, Arnold who was desperately clinging to life in the back seat, and a woman named Jessica who sat unharmed in the driver's seat.

Albert wriggled on the ground like a worm, his hands and feet shackled. Chunks of dirt and gravel clung to his face. He narrowed his eyes at me. I strode over to him and knelt down just above his face. Drops of my subordinates' blood dripped onto the weeds behind me.

"If you had lied to me and never reported a thing to the authorities, we would both be a lot happier right now," I whispered.

He growled under the duct tape and rested his head in the dirt. I patted his cheek.

"We'll talk soon."

I helped Eleanor and Cynthia carry the injured inside, leaving Jessica to guard Albert. We laid Devin and Arnold on a pair of cots near the front door. When Eleanor undid Devin's jacket, I saw that a bullet had destroyed the microphone. I yanked it off of him and stuffed it into my pocket. At least two rounds had hit him. Survival without a hospital stay was unlikely, but after the crime he had just committed, if he were recognized, he and anyone who accompanied him would have been interrogated by hospital staff.

"Albert's injured! If you're going to interrogate him, sooner is better than later," Devin shouted.

Even in his dire condition, his concern rested with the mission at hand. He was a good theocrat. I smiled at him and squeezed his hand.

"You did very well Devin. There will be a special place in heaven for you. Eleanor, help Jessica bring Albert inside. Cynthia, tend to Arnold."

They departed, leaving me alone with Devin.

"Devin, it's very important that you listen to me right now. Did Cynthia get a chance to burn the letter?"

He pondered for a moment, seemingly distracted by pain.

"I don't think so. We were fired upon before she was able to. She probably still has it."

"Thank you. Get some rest. I'll take care of everything else. Vexrus is with you."

That empty platitude seemed to soothe his pain. It was so easy for me to grant him peace in what were most likely his final moments. In reality, of course, this peace was baseless. It was borne of empty jargon from a fraudulent prophet.

"Thanks, Marlow. I'm glad I got to serve the Vexrus First movement."

I wanted to scream. The dying man before me thanked me for reducing him to such a state. There must have been officials in the government that watched similar macabre spectacles day after day, knowing full well that nothing awaited the dead and dying.

I opened my mouth, half expecting to blurt out a confession, but nothing came. As usual, I buried my guilt, composed myself, and returned to the task at hand.

I walked over to Arnold's cot. Cynthia stood over him with a grave expression. I jostled his shoulder and asked for a response, but heard only gargling. Thinking Arnold to be too far gone, I turned my attention to Cynthia.

"Are you okay? Were you injured?"

She shook her head. I needed to know if she read the letter. In it, I explained the order I had given my supporters. I tried to use vague, imprecise language, but I implied that, if Albert attempted the same gamble I had, he would be shot on the spot. If she had discerned that, she was a liability. Her passive response told me little. I needed to press her.

"Just remember, Vexrus is taking care of the others now. They aren't in pain, and soon Arnold won't be either."

I tried to sound reassuring, but she was unresponsive. Was she in shock from what she had just witnessed, or was she silently questioning my authority? I considered inquiring about the letter, but I feared that the others might overhear. Eleanor entered before I could investigate further.

"How're they doing?" she asked.

"I don't think Arnold is going to make it," Cynthia said.

Eleanor looked at the ground and sighed.

"What about Devin?"

"I think he'll be fine if we get him some medical attention," Cynthia said, placing a washcloth on Arnold's forehead.

I then saw an opportunity to solve multiple problems simultaneously.

"Eleanor, you and Jessica drive Devin to the hospital in Karasan. Relis authorities will be all over you if you go to one here."

"Do you think we have time?" Eleanor asked.

"If you take him and leave immediately, yes. Go tell Jessica to pull the car around, and Cynthia, you tend to Albert."

With them occupied, I crept over to Devin, who was slipping in and out of consciousness. I snuck into my room and took a toolbox from a storage closet. Inside, I found a pair of pliers. I ran over to Devin, shoved them into his wound, and clamped down on the first thing I could wrap them around. He looked at me in a daze. Blood loss had dulled his senses. I squeezed as hard as I could, and Devin's face contorted in pain. Something gave and blood poured out of the wound. I wrapped the pliers in a rag, and tossed them into my room.

"Guys, Devin doesn't look too good. We need to hurry!" I shouted while holding a blood-soaked rag against his wound.

They ran back inside and the three of us carried him to the car. His breathing had become labored, and his eyes rolled back. He would surely die before they made it to the hospital, protecting us from investigation, and protecting me from the hazy confessions of a man on painkillers. The chances that the hospital staff would recognize my subordinates as traitors would be slim, but not zero. In the absence of an afterlife, every minor risk needed to be mitigated. We slid him onto the back seat and propped his head up with his folded jacket.

"Eleanor, before you go, can you give me a gun? I may need it in the event that they were followed."

"Sure, just take Arnold's."

She handed me a bloodied pistol and hopped into the passenger seat. She was frantic, too frantic to look for foul play.

They drove away, leaving Cynthia, Albert, and myself. Attempting to tie up loose ends had a nasty tendency to create more, but now I had my final two in front of me without interference.

Chapter 15

Whether or not Eleanor and Jessica walked in on me executing Albert was irrelevant, so I decided to start with Cynthia. She and I had handcuffed Albert's hands behind a support pillar in the middle of the room and patched him up enough to delay death from blood loss. At no point did she mention the letter. It was entirely possible that she had followed my orders and not read it, but there was no way for me to confirm it. I could glean nothing from her behavior, and if I addressed it directly, she may have acted unpredictably. As I had demonstrated, a crisis of faith could catalyze unreasonable actions.

Albert looked sufficiently restrained to be left alone for a few minutes. He oscillated between staring off into space and scowling at me, but did not struggle against his bindings. I did not want to leave Cynthia's corpse anywhere that it could be found by the others if it could be avoided. I took Arnold's bloodied jacket and wrapped it around Albert's head so he wouldn't realize he was alone in the room after we left. He protested beneath the duct tape covering his mouth to no avail. He soon calmed down and stopped squirming. Satisfied that I had pacified him, I motioned to Cynthia to follow me outside. In the moonlight, she looked exhausted. Was she being tormented by the loss of her faith? Did she know I was a fraud? Was she remembering the sight of her colleagues being gunned down earlier that day? I needed to know, but she could not be trusted to tell me.

"Why did you want to go outside?" she asked.

"I just needed some fresh air before talking to him. We have a little bit of history, and I wanted to clear my head first."

I looked her up and down searching for any slight twitch or anxious body language, anything to convey that she was keeping a secret from me. Her mouth quivered for a moment before she spoke again. Was she concerned with making a bad impression on her new prophet or fearful of giving herself away?

"Oh, I almost forgot, I still have the letter," she told me.

She reached into her breast pocket and retrieved a crumpled piece of paper. Much of the writing was visible. If she felt so inclined, she could have read at least part of it without the others noticing.

"Did you read any of it?" I asked, knowing that, regardless of her answer, I had to kill her.

"Of course not. Here, take it," she said, and dropped it into my hands.

I wished I had the luxury of trusting her. If I were a betting man, I would have wagered that she was telling the truth. I looked down at the letter, crumpled it up, and stuffed it into my pocket.

"So, if it's not too personal, why do you think Vexrus picked you?" she asked.

I tried to conjure up an explanation that would satisfy her, one that would put her at ease with me, but what purpose would it serve? She was marked for death the moment she failed to destroy the letter.

"Well, you see---" I started to speak but was interrupted by Albert groaning. He craned his head toward us. Perhaps he could hear us through the crack between the door and doorframe.

"Follow me around back. I don't like eavesdroppers," I said.

She nodded and followed me behind the cabin. The building blocked most of the moonlight, creating a small patch of complete darkness aside from the square of dim light cascading through the cabin's back window. She stood in front of the window watching Albert try to shake the jacket off of his head.

"I doubt he can hear us," she said.

"I think we're perfectly safe back here," I said, trailing my finger along my pistol grip in the dark.

"Why do *you* think Vexrus chose me?" I asked.

She pondered for a moment, studying my silhouette.

"I honestly don't know, but I trust Vexrus' decision," she replied.

It was a reasonable answer. The answer countless citizens would have given. An answer that proved the necessity of her elimination. She and probably everyone else's loyalty lied with Vexrus, or at least the prevailing conceptualization of Him. If a more suitable prophet presented themselves, I would have been cast aside without another thought.

"Vexrus *chose* me because I stopped believing in Him. He *chose* me because I knew that he couldn't refuse. He *chose* me because the State forced me into a position where He had to."

"I don't understand. How could you not believe in Him?"

Her voice quivered.

"Vexrus was never real, Cynthia. I had to choose between lying and dying, and I made my choice."

Her eyes slowly widened, and her breathing quickened. Much like it had done to me, the realization that the State's god was fiction immediately filled her with panic.

"You're lying. You have to be lying!"

I shook my head and drew Arnold's pistol from my jacket pocket.

"I'm not. This is one of the few times recently that I've told the truth to anyone."

She saw the gun in my hand and backed against the window.

"What happens when we die then?"

I looked down at the gun in my hand. It was heavy and stained with Arnold's blood. So much blood had been spilled because of that question.

"I don't know," I said while taking aim at her.

"Why do you want to kill me? Why did you do any of this? You destroyed Visryan," she said.

"You could have read the letter and found me out. I have to put you down before that happens."

"I didn't read the goddamned letter, Marlow."

She began to hyperventilate and mutter to herself under her breath.

"I couldn't have believed you anyway, but it doesn't matter now."

Tears ran down her face.

"Why did you have to tell me? You could've just shot me in the back, and I wouldn't have been afraid to die. You goddamned monster!"

She dropped to her knees, shaking. Between her agonizing screams and dry heaves, I deduced that her faith had been genuine, but I had destroyed it. I felt like a scientist studying a rat in a lab, watching it writhe in pain, tortured by my hand in the pursuit of whatever scrap of information I could find. I felt a tinge of guilt but also removed from the spectacle. I was watching what a loss of faith looks like in another person, one who was as zealous as I had been. I was studying my own condition. In her I saw the fear that would one day come for me when I lay on my deathbed. Confusion, panic, and a gnawing dread. I would one day be punished for what I had done; there was no escaping that. I would live every day trying to avoid becoming the sniffling, miserable person in front of me, but no matter how long I avoided it, it was inevitable. She was no threat to me. I wanted to comfort the pathetic thing I had turned Cynthia into, but there was nothing I could do. The same fear I saw on display here undulated deep inside me, as well, suppressed only by the distance between then and my death.

She pulled herself up and stared at her reflection in the window. I considered asking what she was thinking about then. How did she see herself now that she had been reduced to soulless flesh and bone? But I refused to subject her to any more abuse. Without another word, I shot her three times in the back. Albert yelled something as she fell against the window and slid to the ground. The muzzle flash briefly illuminated her and me. Had I not been the one who reduced her to such a dreadful state, I would have considered shooting her to be an act of mercy. Albert shook like a man possessed. Perhaps he thought that those shots belonged to pro-State personnel who had come to save him, and he was trying to give them his position. I dragged Cynthia's corpse into the woods. After bringing Albert there, the cabin was tainted. An anonymous tip about a bullet-riddled van could give us away. It was wise to move on and leave traces of our crimes, especially mine, behind us. I was sure Eleanor would agree. I nestled Cynthia's body beneath a thorn bush thirty or so feet from the tree line.

Before I left her, I stared at her blank expression in an attempt to find something significant, a sign that she lived on in some capacity or that she found some sort of peace when I shot her. Of course, as expected, I found nothing. Vexrus had given us dignity and meaning in death. Without Him, I saw only a corpse stuffed under a pile of leaves and thorns. I despised the world I had discovered.

I returned to the cabin and wiped the blood splatter from the window. Albert had shaken the jacket from his head and stared at me with a look of horror. I smiled at him and waved. I rubbed my sleeve against the window, but a slight red hue remained. I shrugged and strode around to the front door. I flung it open, slamming it against the wall. I then drew my pistol from my pocket and fired at the window from inside, shattering it.

"Sorry about that. I couldn't clean all of the blood off; so, I needed to break the window," I said.

I walked over to him and inspected my handiwork.

"I had to come in here first. If the window was broken from the outside, it would not only mean that someone shot at us from outside but also the blood on the window would be visible, and that wouldn't make much sense. This way, I can claim that I shot at an unknown assailant that Cynthia then chased into the woods. Tragically, she was gunned down in the line of duty, but she'll be honored for her sacrifice for all eternity."

I bent down and tore the duct tape off of Albert's face.

"That's the kind of lie you tell, right? Scam after scam. How many hoops do you jump through every day to keep everyone convinced?" I asked.

"I figured that there were two possibilities. Either you believed so hard that you convinced yourself that Vexrus somehow spoke to you, or you knew He didn't exist. I guess it's the latter," he said.

"Yeah, it is," I replied.

I dragged an old wooden chair across the floor and sat in front of him. I placed my foot on the windowsill and leaned back.

"You know, the nation is falling apart because of you. People are tearing each other limb from limb in the streets over nonsense, and instead of trying to address that, you kidnapped an old man and gunned down your own supporters. Some prophet you turned out to be."

"I'm trying to stay alive first and foremost. It's not my fault that you and your cronies lied to everyone. *You* made this the only viable option."

He let out a sharp exhale.

"With Vexrus, the people are contented to live in squalor for their entire lives. Without Him, they're violent and afraid. They were a lot better off before, and you were too, weren't you? I mean, that's what you said when I got here."

"Well, now I know, and there's no way to go back."

He laughed a little, studying me.

"It's awful, isn't it? I'm an old man, you know. Even if you don't kill me tonight, I'll die soon, and there's no escaping that. I think about it every day."

"How many people know? Is it just the Scholars?"

He adjusted himself with a groan and watched the wind blow through the trees through the shattered window.

"Well, to be honest, it's pretty rare as best I can tell, though you're right to suspect the Scholars, most if not all of us know. Businessmen, homeless people, celebrities, bureaucrats, anyone can lose their faith. This kind of thing, someone going haywire when they have a crisis of faith, happens once or twice a year in Relis. I'd estimate that there's about fifty per year nationally. The majority are like you: terrified, miserable, and unable to face the world around them. A sizable chunk of them off themselves before we can get to them. Some try to use their discovery to their advantage in one way or another, usually just selling afterlife credit. We find them pretty quickly and put them down like we should have done with you."

"What stopped you? The Department of the Interior had my house bugged. You obviously knew where I was throughout the day. Why wait?"

"The fake name you gave me slowed me down a little, and your performance convinced that agent from the courthouse, Eleanor Riley, I believe. Department of the Interior agents tend to be faithful to a fault; they give too much lee-way to anyone who gushes over the State, like you. We also wanted to see if you would lead us to where you got the books you were talking about. It wasn't until they tossed your apartment that we realized it was the same stuff Reginald Finster had. He told us that he had destroyed them. He was right, actually. We used to print different books for different areas, but stopped for fear of something like this happening. It's hard to keep borders air tight."

"How did this all start?" I asked him. "This system, some-one had to put it in place. The State's narrative says that the first iteration of *The Book of Vexrus* was printed a few hun-dred years ago. There must be some communication be-tween you and the others that know, right? Who decides what god says?"

He threw his head back and laughed.

"Marlow, I have no goddamned idea how it all started. I'm not part of some evil cabal. I figured out that Vexrus wasn't real and wriggled my way into the government like most of the Scholars. This system we're a part of is so much bigger than ourselves. Even while composing the sacred book, we use vague language to obfuscate what we're actu-ally doing for fear of a true believer somehow being present. I have never spoken so frankly about this in my life. Yeah, I guess somebody started it somehow centuries ago, but they lost control of it. As far as I know, there is no central author-ity, only people who exploit the system, like us. Vexrus, or the idea of Him, controls us just as much as we use it to control the masses."

I hated how little he could tell me. There were other people like me, hiding and quietly subsisting on the knowledge they had discovered. At any moment, one of them could challenge Vexrus and ascend to my status.

"So, what was it that set you off? You could have ignored the afterlife credit system forever. It could have been a pretty easy life," he said.

I clenched my jaw.

"How can life be easy when I'm getting closer and closer to oblivion every minute?"

He shrugged.

"It's the situation you're in. Accept it."

I stood, angry at his passive demeanor.

"Do you accept it?"

I pressed the muzzle of my gun against his cheek.

"Are you *really* ready to die right now?" I asked.

He glared at me and shook his head.

"No, and I never will be. If I thought there was anything I could say to get out of this, I would say it."

His breathing had quickened, but aside from that, he remained impressively calm.

"You recommended that I be killed. I would never let you go."

"My recommendation was the correct one," he said and narrowed his eyes.

I scowled and returned the gun to my jacket pocket.

"Had you been killed, the rest of the nation would be thriving! You're just like the unwashed masses: selfish, cowardly. You don't care about the greater good. It's all about that afterlife number ticking higher. People like you remind me why a theocracy is a good system! Some people need their behavior modified or else they'll be a danger to everyone around them."

I stopped to think for a moment. Albert was right. I had caused irreparable damage to the nation in the name of self-preservation. In this new, godless world, my life now revolved around the accumulation of power and the elimination of potentially problematic people. Was it wrong though? *Was anything wrong?* Vexrus was gone. There was little concrete reason to behave in any specific way. Doing that which impeded one's ascension to heaven was once wrong, and that which assisted in one's ascension was once right. Without that incentive in place, what use did I or anyone else have for a moral structure? Besides, who was *he* to talk of morality? He spent his life lying and killing people behind the scenes.

"I'm not going to sit here and be preached at by someone like you, Albert. As far as I'm concerned, you and I are the same. We both survive off of the adoration of people we lie to. Those people out there in the streets aren't killing each other because of me; they're doing it because of Vexrus. If their lives didn't revolve around dying, maybe they'd be a bit more civilized."

Albert looked down at his lap.

"Yeah, maybe," he said.

I checked the time. If I were lucky, I had about twenty minutes until Eleanor returned. I would have liked to converse with this man, my only colleague, until dawn, but I couldn't risk him speaking to the others.

"I'm changing the subject. Why didn't you or anyone else for that matter claim that Vexrus spoke to them?" I asked Albert. "Even if the thought had never crossed your mind, you could've countered me."

"Doing that en masse would just disprove Vexrus' existence, and that would make things worse. Being gunned down by the State for heresy isn't much different from getting torn limb from limb by an angry mob for being a liar. Besides, to be honest, I don't think anyone wants to be in your position. I mean look at you. Blood-splattered all over your clothes, sweating bullets, bags under your eyes, always glancing over your shoulder for any threat, real or imagined, the need to constantly act like god's elect. You're in hell now; tell me, is it any better than oblivion?"

Hell, I could understand. Hell, I could tolerate. Oblivion, my own non-existence, terrified me. The very presence of oblivion as a concept filled me with dread. Of course this was preferable to oblivion, and I would suffer this hellish state to delay the angry mob for as long as possible.

"So, you don't think anyone is going to copy me?"

"I don't know, Marlow, but that's why I didn't. What would you do if they did?"

"I'm going to avoid the issue altogether. Over the next week or so, I'm going to have the Scholars killed off."

His face contorted in disgust.

"You're an animal. You're going to kill hundreds for what, another forty years on Earth if you're lucky? That's assuming you don't say something stupid and get shot by that deranged captain of yours. Besides, you'll never get every non-believer. When someone decides to roll the dice the same way you did, and believe me, thanks to you, someone will, your little empire is gonna crumble. I guess we Scholars were right; oblivion is a powerful motivator."

We were then interrupted by my cell phone ringing. It was Eleanor. I picked up the discarded duct tape and re-covered Albert's mouth.

"Hello," I said, keeping an eye on Albert.

"Marlow, listen. Devin died on the way to the hospital, and we got rid of the body. We're heading back," she said.

I felt guilt but refused to let it affect my performance.

"I'm sorry to hear that. I hope he wasn't in too much pain."

"He was unconscious the entire time. I don't think he felt a thing."

I pushed fragments of bloodied glass off of the windowsill as we spoke.

"When do you think you'll be back?"

"Fifteen, maybe twenty minutes."

"Do you think you could hurry? Cynthia saw some movement in the woods."

"What did it look like? I can have someone out there faster."

I heard her engine rev in the background.

"Send them, and I'm not sure. She went into the woods to investigate. I have to finish speaking with Albert. We'll deal with this soon."

I hung up and tore the duct tape off again. I dropped to my knees in front of him and put my hands on his shoulders.

"I empathize with you. Killing you will be uniquely painful. Most people are elated at their time of death, but you're afraid. I'm sorry, Albert."

I stood back and aimed at his head. His eyes welled, and his breathing quickened. I was right; he was afraid.

"Marlow, if you come out on top and kill every enemy you've concocted, you're going to have an awful lot of control over what the people believe. They need comfort, peace of mind, a reason not to be afraid. Please, once you're lording over the nation from atop a pile of corpses, just make sure Visryan is a State worth serving."

"I am the State," I responded, raising my weapon.

He shook his head and stared at the floor. I pulled the trigger. He fell face down in a puddle of blood partially suspended by his shackles. Arnold's sightless eyes stared blankly

189

at the ceiling; Cynthia lay with worms and insects in the woods; Devin probably sat in some horrid Department of the Interior dumping ground, and I had put them there. Oblivion was a powerful motivator indeed.

Chapter 16

I dropped Arnold's gun and stood in the midst of my atrocity. A slight breeze blew through the shattered window and whisked the scent of gunpowder away. Gradually, nocturnal birds began to chirp again, and small animals began to rustle through the grass. I retreated to my bedroom and turned on the television. I flipped through the various news channels a few times each. It was about eight o'clock— roughly two hours had passed since we had captured Albert, plenty of time for the incident to be reported to the media. The major networks were seemingly unaware of Albert's disappearance. Though, once they were notified, they would probably spend multiple days on the tale of the missing Scholar. As I neared the end of my search, I saw his face plastered on a local Relis news station next to the anchor.

"Our top story tonight, a Scholar kidnapped. Our field reporter James has the details."

They cut to an image of crime scene tape surrounding the Institute of Vexrus Studies. My Vexrus Firsters' bodies lay scattered across the ground, covered by bloodied blankets. I counted the corpses. Five of my subordinates died on the scene, but there were fourteen total. In the background sectioned off by traffic cones, I saw multiple bullet-riddled vehicles belonging both to the Institute as well as the Department of the Interior.

"I'm here at the Institute of Vexrus Studies where earlier today a group of terrorists in an unmarked van kidnapped Albert Woodward, one of Relis' most cherished Scholars. He was dragged into the van while security forces fired on the assailants. Eyewitnesses say that, when security from the Institute got into their cars to chase the terrorists, they were attacked by a rogue contingent of the Department of the Interior. Many of the assailants were former members of the Department of the Interior who deserted after Marlow Wilson's trial earlier this month. It is unclear whether or not these individuals were still affiliated with the organization at this time," he said as images of Arnold, Jessica, Devin, and Cynthia appeared on screen.

"Four of the assailants are believed to still be in the city. Be on the lookout for these potentially dangerous individuals and report them to the authorities."

Neither I nor anyone else had contacted another group for support, to my knowledge. Whoever assisted us had done so of their own accord. Albert said that the members of the Department of the Interior were faithful to a fault. Perhaps more local agents had decided that serving my interests would be a safer path to ascension than serving the State's.

Shouting began to overtake the reporter's audio. He stepped closer to the camera and moved the microphone next to his mouth. He pointed to the left just off screen.

"Protestors have been at the institute for the past hour or so. A few of them have tried to disrupt the investigation."

The camera panned left to show fifty or so screaming citizens holding cardboard signs with phrases such as "he deserved it" and "purge the rest." Support for the State had dropped even more than the media let on.

"Investigators are unsure of what may have motivated this savage attack on one of our beloved Scholars, but we'll keep you updated."

The anchor returned now accompanied by my picture.

"In other news, Marlow Wilson is still nowhere to be found after his chaotic trial. State officials are offering fifteen hundred fully transferrable afterlife credits for information on his location."

I scowled and changed the channel to a different media network. After a few commercials, an older man in a suit appeared.

"Welcome back, ladies and gentlemen. Marlow Wilson is still causing trouble. Last night in Alexandria, protestors demanding a 'purge of corrupt State officials,' as Marlow put it, clashed with State police after a local official decreed that Mr. Wilson was not exonerated from his crimes. This is the third incident of Vexrus Firsters attacking police in the last twenty-four hours. Things are getting so bad, in fact, that the State is threatening to fine protestors fifty points of afterlife credit for showing support for the Vexrus First movement for a first offence. For those who reoffend, the Afterlife Administration has authorized the total revocation of all afterlife credit. That's right; the State considers these people to be such a threat that they'll cut you off from the afterlife. Keep that in mind before you associate with these people. Now with me I have a political analyst who personally witnessed these riots, Miranda Jones."

A line bisected the screen, and a woman appeared beside the host.

"Thank you for having me," she said.

"I always love having loyal, faithful guests like yourself on the show. So, tell me, how can the people regain Vexrus' favor after behaving in such an unsightly way?"

This loaded question conveyed that the State still exercised some power over the media.

"Well, if the goal is to please Vexrus, I think we should start by purging the State of people like yourself. Everyone watching this saw what I saw. Do not listen to these talking heads! They're part of the same---" she vanished from the screen.

"Good god we are so sorry about that, folks. Apparently, we need to vet our guests a little more thoroughly," he laughed nervously and transitioned to an early commercial break.

I had never lashed out against the media. My supporters were so zealous that they found and fought my battles for me. I had planted a conspiratorial seed, and my supporters were making it grow. The State's weakening-but-still-relevant control over the media limited my perspective, but one thing was clear: I was winning.

Through the slit in my bedroom curtains, I saw a pair of headlights turn off of the road and onto the winding path through the grove. I switched off the television, walked into the living room, picked Arnold's gun up off of the floor, and pointed it out of the broken window as if I was searching for a target. Tires screeched and two pairs of boots hit the ground outside, presumably Eleanor and Jessica, but then more followed. I heard multiple doors open through the broken window. Someone ordered the others to wrap around the house and neutralize whatever threats they found. I gradually backed away from the window and into the corner. I worried that capturing Albert may have been too risky. Perhaps State forces had tracked me down. Flashlights shone through the front windows and the doorknob shook. I took aim at the door. It flung open to reveal a man in a trench coat, Department of the Interior uniform, and officer's cap all embroidered with five gold bars. He was an imposing man with an angular face and knowing gaze.

"There's no need to shoot me. We're on the same side; Eleanor contacted me," he held up his hands and instructed his subordinates to do the same. "My name is Edward

Johansen, and I am the head of Relis' Department of the Interior branch."

I put the gun in my pocket and breathed a sigh of relief. Through the broken window, I saw agents peering into the woods with their flashlights. Edward walked over to me and stared at Albert. He shook his head and grimaced.

"It's a damn shame," he said and turned towards me.

I was unsure of what to say. This man far outranked Eleanor. It was possible that he was one of the few aware of Vexrus' non-existence.

"You know, I've worked with Albert for a long time. He always seemed like a good, pious man. I honestly thought that he wanted what was best for the State. Do you think he was always abusing his position or that something turned him later in life?" he asked.

"To be perfectly transparent, I don't really know. I'm just a mouthpiece; the orders I've given came straight from Vexrus."

He nodded, seemingly satisfied, and turned his attention to his subordinates outside. I felt it wise to portray myself as just a pawn. Doing so might excuse me if I said something particularly egregious or gave a stupid order. Ironically, by presenting myself in this manner, my influence grew stronger. Any failure could be excused by claiming that it must have been part of an even greater plan.

"You guys see anything?" he shouted.

"There's some blood splattered in the grass over here," one agent said.

"There's a trail leading this way. It looks like someone was being dragged," said another.

Edward tilted his head.

"Marlow, what exactly happened here?"

"I was interrogating Albert with the help of another Department of the Interior agent who is loyal to the cause, Cynthia. She thought she heard something outside, so she went to investigate. Right after that, I saw two silhouettes in the light coming through the window at the tree line. Aside from Cynthia and myself, there were no other allies in the area. I fired on them from inside. One of them grabbed their shoulder afterwards and ran off, followed by the other. That's when I called Eleanor."

"And where is Cynthia?"

"She never came back. She may have chased them when they fled."

Moments later, two of Edward's subordinates stopped in the woods at the thorn bush where I had left Cynthia. One of them bent down and began to look over her remains. The pair then sprinted to the window.

"Sir, we found a body. It's a woman, fairly young, wearing a Department of the Interior uniform."

I tried to look distraught. I nodded and buried my face in my hands.

"That's probably Cynthia."

"Hm, that's unfortunate. She's with Vexrus now though. Did you hear any gunshots or anything after she went outside?"

"It was hard to hear anything over Albert's screaming. He was pretty uncooperative."

Another pair of agents dragged her up to the window. I looked at the floor, uninterested in seeing my handiwork again.

"It looks like she was shot in the back," one of them said.

"Makes sense. They were waiting for her. Well, there's no helping it now. Bring her in here and get ready to torch this place," Edward said.

"Torch it? Why would you do something like that?" I asked.

"Tying up loose ends. Who knows what the State could do with a scrap of paper or a dead person's forgotten cell phone," Edward answered calmly. "When the stakes are as high as they are, you have to be extremely careful."

"I understand."

I was relieved. I would have soon ordered the cabin to be burned to cover my tracks regardless. Eleanor then burst through the door and ran up to me.

"Marlow, we need to get out of here," she said quickly. "Commander Johansen has an armored personnel vehicle and an escort. No one will be able to touch us."

She took a quick look at Albert and motioned for me to follow her. Rows of agents lined either side of my path as I walked from the cabin to the personnel carrier. There must have been over seventy agents present, along with millions of dollars' worth of equipment. One of them even held a riot shield up behind me while I climbed into the back. Its steel walls must have been at least three inches thick. I sat down on a long metal bench, and was accompanied by a handful of what I assumed were my supporters. Many of them stared at me in awe, mouths agape. I said hello and sat down. Eleanor sat across from me, and someone slammed the door from outside. Almost immediately, the engine roared to life, and we pulled away from the cabin.

"Are you injured?" Eleanor asked.

"No, I'm okay, but if you haven't already heard, Cynthia didn't make it."

She nodded and exhaled sharply through her nose.

"I know. She died doing the right thing and knew it. I'm sure she's being celebrated right now."

She wiped a tear from the corner of her eye and smiled as if to reassure me. I smiled back, my stomach churning. She then pointed to the people lining the benches.

"What do you think of our new Vexrus Firsters? The Department of the Interior is falling apart, and the disaffected agents love you. We have some of them to thank for helping us catch Albert."

The starstruck agent next to me nodded his head.

"The fact of the matter is, damn near every agent in Relis is either on our side, or they've been shot by one who is. You wouldn't see it online or on the news, but the State is seriously struggling to maintain power in the city. It's quite possible that you're the most powerful person in the region," Eleanor said.

"We're heading to the Department of the Interior headquarters right now. When we get away from here, we'll open the windows and let you have a look. It's quite a sight," the man next to me said.

"Are you sure the city is safe? They're hunting me there, you know," I replied.

"What are they going to do? They don't have any influence there anymore, especially not in the Department of the Interior regional headquarters. If a random citizen was given a gun and told to shoot you with it, odds are they would turn on whoever gave it to them. Not to mention, you're with us. No one is gonna touch you," he said.

"When Jessica and I were driving to Karasan, it was chaos. Riot police lined the city; had Devin held on longer, we still probably wouldn't have been able to get through the blockade," Eleanor said. "The violence is definitely escalating."

The movement was growing beyond myself; I wondered who my followers would target when left to their own devices, given the vagueness of my conspiracy. They were a ravenous, angry mob in search of a target. I had to direct their ire before it destroyed the nation.

The driver tapped on the metal grid separating the back of the vehicle from the cab.

"We're entering the city. See for yourself," he said.

One of the agents slid a piece of metal aside to reveal a small rectangular window with metal grating. I sat on my knees and pressed my face against it. Piercing emergency sirens echoed through the mostly barren streets. There were no riot police to be found, nor any State police forces of any kind. Burning cars sat on the side of the street unattended. The few people I saw were looting what little remained in the shops lining the sidewalk. The State-owned buildings we passed were in far worse condition. They had been reduced to piles of smoldering cinders and picked clean of anything of use. In the shattered window of what had once been a police station, I saw a ragged banner swaying in the wind. On it was a crown not unlike the ones on Visryan's flag, set against a bright red background. This time, however, there was only one, and it was labeled "Vexrus." Spraypainted on the concrete underneath was written "purge heretical rulers." It was not the only one I saw. Others hung from office windows and defaced monuments. The letters "V.F.M." appeared on many of them. The agents told me that it was the movement's new insignia.

Near the center of town, flurries of embers and plumes of smoke filled the skies. A man in a bloodied coat sitting on the side of the road drinking water waved at us as we passed. Some citizens cheered, some clapped, but servants of the

State ran. The crowd gradually grew denser the further we went, forcing us to slow to a crawl. I heard a muffled megaphone echoing from somewhere in front of us. A woman cleaned a man's wounds in an alley. A group of teenagers distributed makeshift knives to anyone who would take one. A trio sporting the insignia on their backs filled a bag with chunks of concrete broken off from the sidewalk. One of them picked up a few handfuls and ran ahead of us, jumping over downed power lines along the way. We caught up with them moments later and screeched to a halt. I could now hear the megaphone clearly.

"This is a direct order from the Supreme Council. Stand down immediately, or you will be shot. Any offenders that die here today are to be damned upon death without exception. Ask yourself, are you truly willing to bet your eternity on the actions of a deranged murderer?" a man said in a booming voice.

The Vexrus Firster began hurling the blocks of concrete they'd gathered at the State troops just out of view in front of us.

"His will be done" sounded through the megaphone, followed by a gunshot.

The remaining rocks slid out of their hand and clacked across the asphalt, and they fell backward, dead. I gagged a little. I had inspired someone to undertake such a futile, meaningless act.

"Exit the vehicle at once," the State official said.

"Is he talking to us?" Eleanor asked.

"Looks like it. He ain't so special; we've got a megaphone, too!" the driver shouted back at us.

He retrieved it from somewhere under his seat and rolled down his window.

"We are former agents of the Department of the Interior, now agents of the Vexrus First movement. We have jurisdiction in this region and demand safe passage," he said.

"The Relis branch of the Department of the Interior has been branded a heretical organization by the State as has the Vexrus First movement; both are considered to be in open rebellion. Exit the vehicle immediately and you will be questioned. You have one minute to comply."

The driver quickly made a call and mumbled something. Within seconds, I heard gunshots sound from every direction. Department of the Interior vehicles pulled up beside us one after another, each with a squad of heavily armed agents. Through the metal grid, I saw retaliatory bullets impact the bulletproof windshield of the rebellion official's vehicle, spreading cracks across it. By the time our minute had expired, the police blockade had been annihilated. I was no longer skeptical of our safety. The Vexrus First movement had the State outgunned, at least in Relis. A chorus of cheers sounded from behind us. Vexrus Firsters stood on the side of the street waving banners and shouting their thanks. We resumed driving and passed by what had once been the blockade. Their vehicles were covered in dents and scratches. They had been repelling my supporters for quite a while.

They were the only relevant opposition we faced. Whenever we came to more police forces, they threw their weapons down and ran from us. One even tossed his badge into a storm drain. Whether they had been converted or simply recognized the insurmountable odds mattered little. The police were no longer willing to serve the State.

Chapter 17

Even when I worked for the State, I had not been allowed to enter the Department of the Interior Regional Headquarters. The building was a fortress. A foot-and-a-half thick stone wall topped with razor wire wrapped around the entirety of the property. There was a single heavily surveilled entrance and exit point with around-the-clock guards. Unsurprisingly, these fortifications safeguarded it from damage during the recent civil unrest. Aside from the Vexrus First insignia haphazardly painted on the walls, it looked the same as it had a month ago. A car sped past the rest of our convoy, stopping just in front of the gate. Through the nearly shattered windshield glass, I saw Edward step out of the car and converse with a guard. Shortly after, the gate slid open, and we pulled inside. The interior was immaculate. Elaborate water fixtures, elegant topiary, and lush green grass covered the property. The building at the center resembled something from a historical text. Massive marble pillars holding up a pediment depicting Vexrus handing the sacred book to a State official stood in front of the well-guarded entrance.

We passed a few crumbled statues with shattered faces. I squinted to make out the name written under one of them. I didn't recognize them, but they had apparently been a member of the Supreme Council. Far in the distance up against the interior of the wall, I saw six corpses hanging from gallows.

"What happened to them?" I asked.

"They, like the rest of us, had a choice to make: stand with the State, or stand with Vexrus. They made the wrong one," one of the agents said.

The personnel carrier stopped next to the stairs leading up to the entrance. Metal groaned, and the door swung open to reveal a smiling Edward.

"I'm sure you've spent enough time in that dingy thing," he said. "Come on out and get some fresh air."

I and the others stepped outside into a bizarrely peaceful scene entirely separated from the violence through which we had just driven. Birds chirped and splashed in a fountain against the orange glow of a burning city. In the distance, I saw a towering building tilt gradually faster before toppling over and out of view. Any sound it made was drowned out by distance and the faint wail of a siren far away.

"You're supposed to speak with the other Vexrus First leadership today, right?" Edward asked, pulling me from my daze.

"Yeah, around eleven o'clock. Have you been speaking with them?"

"We have secure lines of communication open with all of them inside. You can talk via video chat."

"I've been meaning to ask, what exactly happened to the Department of the Interior? Eleanor, her subordinates, and I escaped into the woods immediately after our trial. All we've seen is whatever is on the news."

"The Department of the Interior prides itself on hiring exceptionally faithful citizens. We were each vetted for months before joining. The State knew that we sided with Vexrus first and them second. Until you came along, there was no reason to think that those two could ever be at odds with one another. Each of us swore an oath to enact Vexrus' will on earth, and if the State stands in the way of that, it must be overthrown. Other regions as well as ours have already carried out internal purges. I'm confident that everyone on these grounds right now is loyal to Vexrus. The Department of the Interior is gone, replaced by the Vexrus First movement."

Ironically, the agency designed to be unquestionably loyal to the State had been turned against it through the same mechanism the State once used to control it. He started up the stairs and motioned for me to follow. An employee of the Department of Public Spending would never have been able to walk up these stairs unless they were in shackles defending themselves from a criminal accusation or receiving some kind of award.

"Now, Marlow, I have a question for you. What exactly is this conspiracy you're talking about? Who is it and why?" Edward asked.

"Full disclosure: I am not privy to every aspect of Vexrus' plan. What I know for sure is this: certain powerful interests have been misrepresenting Vexrus' will for their own gain and must be removed from power, the primary group in question being the Scholars. Many in the Supreme Council also facilitate the Scholars' lies. I will soon generate a list of targets. It's quite possible that Visryan is rotten to the core."

He nodded and rubbed his chin.

"I knew that the Scholars were corrupt the moment they pushed for a bounty on your head. The Supreme Council allowed it to happen. Either they're too blind to see the truth, or they're actively trying to suppress it. Whichever is the case, they're not fit to rule," he replied.

The Scholars had been quietly pushing for my elimination the entire time. The news spoke of a fifteen-hundred afterlife credit bounty on my head. Maybe the Scholars wanted whoever captured or killed me to die shortly after. That would explain why they offered the exact amount needed to ascend. If I were in their position, Marlow's killer would have been made to commit suicide regardless.

"Agreed," I said.

Etched into the walls and on the underside of the pediment were the faces of countless State officials, most of them famous. One face in the center of a wall labeled *Our Scholars* had been shattered.

Once inside, I was immediately surrounded by starstruck Vexrus Firsters. A few of them dropped to their knees and cried when they saw me. They were in a state of religious ecstasy. Edward put up a hand to halt their approach.

"Now, I know you're all very happy that Marlow is alright, but we have to be a little more professional than that. When the work is done, maybe you can ask a question or two."

They saluted us and dispersed, some wiping the tears from their eyes. On every wall was etched a long-winded creed to which each of them swore. A couple of agents were in deep meditation in front of the walls, presumably contemplating the divinity of Vexrus.

"They were concerned that we would be too late to rescue you," he said with a nervous laugh.

"I'm flattered, really."

He led me to an elevator and sent us to the top floor.

"Where is Eleanor?" I asked.

"Resting, probably. Don't you worry about her. She'll be getting a promotion as well as her weight in awards."

"I was wondering if she could be placed in charge of my security detail," I said.

"I suppose that could be arranged, but it seems like a waste of someone who would better serve the State as a higher-ranked officer."

I hated the thought of losing such a loyal subordinate. I wanted someone who I knew beyond a shadow of a doubt would die for me if called upon. Despite the divinely ordained, cosmically significant position society at large believed me to occupy, I only wanted to delay the inevitable. In reality, little had changed since I worked for the State. My life still revolved around running from oblivion. The only difference was that now I knew my fight was a futile one.

"It is very likely that attempts will be made on my life. Her skillset proved invaluable while we were in hiding. Standard security forces won't suffice. I'll need a proper, dedicated security team, one that I envision her leading."

"No problem. I'm sure she would be grateful for such a prestigious position."

The elevator opened with a ding to reveal a luxurious room staffed with Vexrus Firsters. A mahogany table with meticulously carved wooden statues resting on it sat in front of pristine leather couches. The marble floors were nearly reflective. A citizen toiling away in a low-paying, low-afterlife-point-yield job would have never been able to afford anything of this magnitude, yet they were far happier than I. The couches faced a massive window overlooking the entire compound. From there, I could see some of Relis, or at least what remained of it. The fire lapping at the sides of towers undulated between red and orange.

"What's the news saying about all this?" I asked.

"See for yourself." He said, pointing to a television remote sitting on a table next to me.

I turned on a television mounted to a wall and changed to the local news. The anchor that had announced the bounty on my head earlier sat next to footage of today's civil unrest playing in a window next to them.

"Has Relis fallen? State officials say that this is simply a temporary heretical incident and promise to restore order as soon as possible. Tonight, we'll be going over some safety tips to help you and your family stay safe during this difficult time."

"That's a load of shit, don't worry. The State is hemorrhaging money and resources trying to stop the rioting. Soldiers are even being recalled from overseas, but I have a feeling that they won't care for the State much once they learn of what's happened. I bet the Supreme Council has local news stations saying that all over the country. It maintains the illusion of authority, and sometimes that's all you need. Sure, that'll keep some people in line, for a while, but eventually, the cracks start to show," Edward said.

His knowledge of the ins and outs of Visryan's public institutions impressed me, but I worried that such a knowledgeable man may somehow see through me. How long could someone who seemingly had eyes and ears everywhere go without coming into contact with another heretic brave enough to challenge god? In the long term, I understood him to be a danger to me, but for the time being, I needed him.

"The police are essentially powerless in Relis now, correct?" I asked.

"More or less. There are some isolated pockets of State influence, but the never-ending waves of civilians attacking them will wipe them out soon."

"And what about the Institute of Vexrus Studies?"

"It's suffered substantial damage. It was a focal point of much of the rioting, but they have well-armed security forces."

"If it isn't gone by tonight, I'd like you to burn it."

Ordering the annihilation of other liars did not carry the same moral weight my other murders had. They and I both subsisted on the adoration of the ignorant masses. They killed countless citizens to maintain their grasp on power. If anything, meeting their end at the hands of State death troopers was poetic justice.

"Consider it done."

He displayed no reservations about annihilating Visryan's most celebrated public servants. It seemed that he had wholeheartedly cast his lot with me.

"And one more thing. Present this news station as well as others that support the State with an ultimatum: either cease programming at once or join the Vexrus First movement. It's entirely possible that the State is forcing them to denounce us. Let them know that they don't have to worry about that anymore."

"And if they refuse?"

"Ensure that they don't."

He gave me an understanding smile and whispered something into an official's ear. The official then motioned to a couple of his colleagues and they exited the room.

"Taken care of, sir." Edward said.

I strode over to the window and stared at *my* city. I wondered how many people hiding from the blaze boarded up in their homes were plotting against me. Surely, a number of statists remained. Anti-Vexrus First media would keep them eternally in the State's service. These people were a threat. I needed to control the flow of information the way the State had once done. Much like Vexrus' existence, my status as His speaker needed to become a fact of life, something not even discussed in public discourse. What color is the sky? Blue. Who is god's elect? Marlow Wilson, of course. Once I controlled the flow of information, my paranoia would subside, and I could at last use my power to bring peace to the nation. The people down there dodging rocks, bullets, and flames should have been grateful. Their new, merciful leader had no plans to inflict the unimaginable misery he suffered through upon them. I envied them, I pitied them, and they disgusted me simultaneously. I felt so far above them as well as those around me. I agonized over forbidden knowledge they would never have to endure. They simply had to function in their day-to-day lives, their fear of death doused by the ultimate opiate. The weight of my knowledge set me apart from them. I felt that it justified my rule. The people themselves argued that they needed divine governance. That much had been made clear from the rioting. They needed a service, and I could provide it. I was a martyr who would selflessly suffer in their stead. Unbeknownst to them, I had given them the greatest gift one could possibly give another: blissful ignorance, and for this, I felt that they owed me at least their obedience.

I had the supporters, political capital, and the will to do what needed to be done. I fished my phone from my pocket and saw that it was nearly time for my meeting with the Vexrus First leadership.

"Edward, would you mind clearing everyone else out of the room. It's nothing personal, but I only want the leadership present for this meeting."

Upon hearing me, the others filed out of the room before Edward had the chance to give them the order.

"Oh, and would you please bring Eleanor, too?"

He looked somewhat perplexed but agreed, and left down the elevator to fetch her. In case Edward had any underlying, well-concealed loyalty to the State or the Scholars, I needed trustworthy security. I turned away from the window and my burning city. From these scorched ruins littered with the bodies of my supporters and detractors alike would rise a new Visryan, one nearly uniform in its belief. A theocracy with only a single non-believer, its ruler.

Chapter 18

I sat at a desk facing a large monitor. The screen was divided into sixteen squares where the leaders of each sect of the Vexrus First movement would appear. I heard the elevator door slide open and looked to see Edward and Eleanor. They stood behind me while one face, then another, then another appeared on screen. Each person looked elated when they saw me. They were reaping the fruits of their labor, finally speaking with their exalted leader.

"Hello everyone. I'm glad you all could attend," I said in the most authoritative tone I could muster.

They greeted me, one of them even referred to me as "your holiness."

"I will try to keep this brief as I know you all have a lot of work to do. In short, the established theological authorities have been deliberately misleading the Visryan people for their own gain. These individuals have no regard for Vexrus' will, and some of them may even be non-believers as this would explain their immoral behavior. It may come as a shock to many of you that the primary group in question is the Scholars. It seems that, despite the trust Vexrus has placed in them, they subvert His will at every turn. They even generate fake books to serve their own ends overseas. They think so little of good people like you. They'll march you into oblivion to line their pockets."

I paused to allow them to gasp. By then, many of them had likely heard of what happened to Albert Woodward and may have been expecting such an order. I scanned the screen, searching for signs of reluctance. A few of them cast their eyes at the ground, but no one protested.

"Many of Visryan's largest, most important cities are represented here today, cities which house various Institutes of Vexrus Study. The majority of these currently house one or two Scholars. You are to eliminate these people without warning. Do not allow them to speak, and do not give them the opportunity to plead their cases. Kill them on sight," I ordered.

I paused again to search for dissent. A few of them appeared increasingly conflicted. The woman with whom I had spoken on the phone earlier winced. They disliked my order, but they were willing to carry it out. Edward put his hand on my shoulder and stepped into view.

"I know it's a challenging order, but remember why we're doing all of this. It's necessary for the success of Visryan," he explained.

A few of them nodded in agreement upon hearing Edward.

"We here in Arlinton are ready to do whatever is necessary, Mr. Wilson," one of them said. "I guarantee it."

The others echoed the same sentiment. Even the leaders who looked away when told of the Scholars' treachery seemed reassured. Despite my divinely ordained power, Edward carried a type of authority I did not. He was respected for his accomplishments, not being chosen by a deity for seemingly arbitrary reasons.

"I'm glad to hear it. The next order of business is the correction of statist media outlets. In our region, we've noticed that most televised content favors the State. A local Relis news outlet even offered a fifteen-hundred afterlife point bounty for my head. You all must instruct companies peddling State propaganda to alter their content as necessary to promote moral behavior and belief. Tell them that it is safe to do so, and that they are no longer under oppressive State management. Mobilize tonight. Confront them at their homes if you have to. We must break the State's hold over the flow of information. If the people aren't exposed to this drivel, they'll realize how illogical, perhaps even heretical, it is to doubt my message."

"Local coverage hasn't been generally positive, but as time passes, it's starting to favor us more, at least in Karasan," one of them said.

"That's how it's been here, too. The cracks are becoming visible, but I think a clean break would be best. Allowing their narrative to persist will bring trouble in the form of radicalized heretics," I insisted.

"Agreed. The longer we allow statist media to operate uncontested, the better chance they'll have to concoct a convincing lie to discredit us," the Arlinton representative said.

"The further they get backed into a corner, the faster they'll resort to radical courses of action. We can't allow it to escalate," said another.

"I couldn't agree more. Be thorough; destroy any communications and broadcasting equipment we can't make use of," I said. "Ensure that they can't preach to hidden heretics waiting to destabilize our new, fragile government."

Someone else challenging Vexrus would be problematic, but that challenge being broadcast would be deadly. I had to keep the media on a short leash. Any rebellious would-be atheist with access to a camera could ruin me if they found an outlet willing to give them a platform. I aimed to make this an impossibility though heavy State regulation. My government would be given at least twenty-four hours' notice before anything was to be aired. Limiting internet communications would come next.

"Okay, everyone. Do what you have to. I trust your judgment. If you have any issues, notify me as soon as possible," I said.

"Wait, Mr. Wilson, I have an important question. Are our afterlife credits still good? Can we still go to heaven with them?" one of them said as I moved to disconnect.

I bit my lower lip to contain a smile. I looked at their expectant faces and exhaled sharply.

"To be honest, I'm not sure if they could have gotten you into the afterlife in the first place, but I know what will. These next few weeks will be the most important of your lives. How you behave now, in this crucial historical moment, will impact where you'll spend eternity more than that number ever did. Do what has to be done, and you will be rewarded."

They looked determined. I had returned to them the prospect of eternity, and they did not intend to disappoint.

"Thank you so much, Mr. Wilson. Thank you for saving me from oblivion," he said and signed off.

It was statements such as these that flung me between self-loathing and delusions of grandeur. He thanked *me*. Not Vexrus, nor the State, Marlow Wilson. Many of them looked teary-eyed. They each vanished one by one, leaving me alone with Eleanor and Edward. I stood and stretched. Edward started to speak, but was interrupted by his ringing phone. He excused himself to answer it, leaving me alone with Eleanor. She had a glistening new medallion pinned to her chest, presumably the first of many Edward had mentioned. Without warning, she hugged me. I patted her back.

"Thank you for giving me a second chance," she said with a tone of sincere appreciation. "You could have killed me with the others. I would've deserved it with the way I treated you, but you spared me."

The power I exercised over how my subordinates viewed reality, regardless of how misplaced it may have been, was intoxicating. I wondered if Vexrus, had He been real, would have felt the same way when looking at one of His zealots.

"You were loyal to Vexrus. Even when you were taunting me in my jail cell, I could see that you weren't conspiring against god," I told her. "You wanted to serve your nation and its people, and that's noble."

"Thank you, Marlow."

She stepped back and wiped her eyes. I looked over at the window. The fires were dying down. Soon, we would know who had survived and who had been swallowed up in the chaos. I did not yet know if I would take credit for having the Scholars killed publicly; perhaps they died as a consequence of their disobedience to god, swallowed up by fire, killed by the will of the cosmos.

Edward returned with a smile stretched across his face.

"Excellent news. We sent a couple of squads to hunt down Relis' remaining Scholars, and they said they'll have them before dawn," he said.

"I can't wait to see what the city looks like tomorrow," said Eleanor, who was sitting on the couch staring out at the plume of smoke.

"Speaking of tomorrow, I'm sure you must be exhausted," Edward said, looking at me. "We have a bedroom set up for you on this floor. Go down the hallway next to the elevator and take the last left."

I thanked him and left for my room. I looked back over my shoulder and saw Eleanor fighting to stay awake watching Relis, the city she had sworn to protect, burn to the ground supposedly for its own good. She was watching the world be remade by god's hand, quite possibly the most significant event in the history of mankind. I wanted to know how it felt to be an instrumental part of the greatest theological revolution in modern history, instead of its greatest scam. I felt remorse for the millions of otherwise good people I had driven to commit violence in god's name. Perhaps, this was the natural progression of a theocracy. Perhaps, I was but the most recent in a long line of heretics. I told myself someone had to hold the reins. If it wasn't me lying to the populace, it would be a Scholar or a member of the Supreme Council. I wasn't some rare malfunction of theocratic governance; I was the logical end product. A heretic destined to rule over the faithful.

Chapter 19

That night, all across the nation, Scholars were awoken in the night, dragged into the streets, and executed without trial to the thunderous applause of onlookers. The Institutes of Vexrus Study held out for a while. Entryways were barricaded with the meaningless wrought iron iconography that had once been used to inspire faith in countless field trip groups and tourists. One of my subordinates showed me a video of the Scholars' security throwing boxes of the sacred book at our forces from a window after they had run out of ammunition. In the capital, a Scholar, upon seeing the growing crowd of onlookers, pled for assistance, claiming that to stand idly by "while our nation was usurped by evil" was to defy god's will. His audience agreed and moments later stormed the building and threw him from a fifth story window. In only a couple of weeks, the scholars had lost absolute power, and I had taken it.

An old man who had spent his life lying to the nation sat in a dank basement behind a barricaded door while the last adherents to the old Visryan deserted or died in the line of duty. He would have heard the melee draw gradually closer. Maybe when they began to pry his door open, he would take his own life, preferring a self-inflicted bullet wound to the humiliation he would face at the hands of the furious masses. If I were this hypothetical Scholar, I would wait. I would let them take me, and I would beg for my life regardless of how futile the effort may have been. I would fear both oblivion and god. Perhaps fear of a god other than Vexrus kept the Scholars from doing what I had done. Perhaps they feared the judgment of some yet-unobserved being.

Dissenting media outlets were raided one after another, as well. I awoke around four in the morning and turned on the television in my room. Most of the channels I flipped through were no longer broadcasting. The few that were on air were begging for State assistance. Some claimed that we were witnessing the end of days. I stopped and watched as a woman who struggled to hold back tears gave me a play-by-play of the raid taking place at her station. The veneer of mainstream media was nowhere to be found, though her speech still had the stilted, sterile tone of a reporter. She heard boots on the first floor, then the second, and once they had reached the third, their footsteps were audible through the television. A door then slammed against the wall off-camera, and she ran out of view. I heard a couple of gunshots before the connection was terminated. Another station still broadcasted through a cracked camera that had been knocked onto the floor. There were no media personalities present, only the euphoric chants of my supporters gathering in the streets around the desecrated building. Another abandoned newsroom streamed the vacated set as fire slowly consumed it. The flames crept toward the Visryan flag they used as a backdrop when the signal finally gave out.

As channels turned to static and monuments to the State turned to ash, the beliefs one could hold publicly changed. The Visryan flags that once flew over every State-owned institution were replaced with the Vexrus First insignia. Overnight, the nation metamorphosed into something that was simultaneously a clone of its former iteration and something entirely different, at least in the minds of the faithful. Loyal media outlets proclaimed that we had entered a new era. The reign of Marlow Wilson, Vicar of Vexrus, god's elect on Earth. They showed footage of the rapture in the streets. Millions dropped to their knees, teary eyed, and thanked Vexrus for allowing them to see such an amazing revolution. They were overcome by the glory of their god, or perhaps their monarch. A smile stretched across my face, illuminated by the glow of the television screen. A short meeting and a few words with the right people were all it took for me to reshape a nation. I was a fearful soulless husk alone in the cosmos, yet I held absolute power.

By dawn, one could not find an anti-Vexrus First broadcast airing anywhere in the nation. I switched the television off and walked down the hall to where the video conference had taken place. I looked down on the city and saw that, aside from a few columns of smoke, likely emanating from targets I had personally designated for destruction, the city was returning to normalcy. The soft glow of early morning hung on the skyline, silhouetting what buildings remained but hiding the damage in the streets. Satisfied that my work was done, I retired to my room for a shower.

The warm water relaxed my muscles as Vexrus Firsters piled Scholars and their loyalists into a mass grave in some undisclosed location. Perhaps the State deserved a fate such as this. After all, Visryan was founded on a lie. A theocracy frail enough to collapse from one televised speech would have eventually done so with or without me. The State that had once seemed so eternal and rigid had always been on the cusp of ruin. Faith created the illusion of supremacy. I now had to generate this illusion. My duty was to set up cardboard entities that appeared so threatening and absolute that those looking at them never realized how insubstantial they actually were. My actions had proven that no amount of military power alone could control the populace. I needed to teach them to regulate their own behavior. It was in their own best interest. Would it not have been crueler to abandon them to oblivion? Actions that could potentially lead one to question their belief in Vexrus needed to be regulated or banned outright. This realization rationalized many of Visryan's policies. If Vexrus was, as the State asserted, an omnipotent super being, then why should His people have feared traveling overseas? What purpose did a national restriction of external travel serve? My earlier, faithful self never understood this. He followed this rule only because failure to do so may have impacted his afterlife credit. Now, I understood that this was intended to prevent us from interacting with individuals that could disprove our faith, or keep us from finding evidence that would do such, like Reggie's books had done with me.

I stepped out of the shower and looked at myself in the mirror. The dark circles underneath my eyes were a recent phenomenon. I brushed my teeth and felt clean for the first time in weeks. Marlow the faithful showered under a security camera. Marlow the heretic enjoyed his own private quarters, and there was no god to levy a moral judgment on either one. Whoever drafted faith-maintaining legislation such as the international travel restrictions was likely privy to the truth. Concocting a narrative that would simultaneously allow me to have them killed while strengthening these restrictions would be a difficult but necessary step to ensuring my safety. Anyone involved in the production of *The Book of Vexrus* could be a liability, as well. Those *proofs* originated from somewhere. The eradication of the Scholars as a class would likely eliminate many of the people with this knowledge. I would erect a wall of corpses between myself and the inevitable. The State taught me to fear nothing more than oblivion, and this fear led me to conquer it.

I dried myself off and returned to my room to search for clothes. I was so tired the night before that I had not thought of what I would wear the next morning. I slid the closet door open to reveal a modified Department of the Interior uniform. Shiny golden buttons, a pair of white gloves, and the word "Vicar" embroidered in gold on the right breast pocket. On the left was the Vexrus First insignia. I got dressed and walked out of my room into a cacophony of ringing phones and the tapping of keyboards. Vexrus Firsters were scattered all over the room, analyzing breaking news from across the country. A couple of them waved but were too busy to speak with me. I walked to the window and stared at the smoldering gray pile Relis had become. It looked war-torn when exposed to sunlight. I opened the window a little to listen for any sounds, but there was only silence. Yesterday's sirens and muffled gunshots were nowhere to be found. Not even the familiar piercing wail of ambulances and car horns had persisted, only unsettling stillness. I checked the clock hanging on the wall and saw that it was nearly time for the morning news.

"Would you all mind if I turned on the television?" I asked the people sitting on the couch behind me.

"Not at all, sir," one of them said and handed me the remote.

Many of the popular media networks still showed only a black screen, but I was searching for my supporters. My subordinates had done their job well. Surprisingly, one local news station was still up and running. An anchor that had lamented the state of the nation less than twenty-four hours prior now sat in front of the Vexrus First insignia with a smile stretched across his face.

"Good people of Visryan. I am ecstatic to report that our station as well as many others are no longer censored by the State. The Vexrus First movement has liberated us. We are now free to report true, accurate news that properly glorifies Vexrus and reinforces moral behavior. Please disregard any anti-Vexrus First or anti-Marlow content we have produced as of late. Such content was created at the behest of the State, and we were threatened with a reduction in afterlife credit if we failed to comply. We will now be delivering announcements on behalf of the movement. As always, our mission is bringing you the truth; now, we have the ability to do so. With that said, let's get to the news. Today's top story: the end of the Scholars. Marlow Wilson, the True Vicar, denounced the Scholars as liars at Vexrus' request. Accordingly, the Vexrus First movement raided multiple Institutes of Vexrus Study, as well as Scholars' homes, to eliminate the threat. A speaker for the movement told us that the majority of Scholars have been killed. If you encounter a former Scholar, you are advised to report the sighting to Vexrus First officials. You can find them at former Department of the Interior buildings and reach them at the Department of the Interior hotline until the transitional period ends. Officials even hinted that doing so could have a positive impact of your afterlife chances."

Salvaging at least part of the afterlife credit system seemed to be a necessity. Citizens needed a metric to track their progress. It was difficult to assign value to any activity without measuring its impact on eternity. I changed the channel to a national media outlet and was pleased to see our insignia sitting next to their logo in the corner.

"So, what you're saying is, the people are happy but confused?" a political pundit asked.

"That's right, Pat. Nearly one hundred percent of those polled said that they have absolute faith in Marlow Wilson. There isn't a question about whether or not he is fit to rule. The question on many citizens' minds is whether or not their afterlife credit is still good. Many people who have faithfully served the State for ten, twenty, or even thirty years want to know if they're still going to be rewarded."

The Vexrus Firsters sitting on the couch looked up at me. They, like the rest of the nation, wanted to know where they stood.

"Of course, faithful service will still be rewarded. Can one of you get me in touch with our loyal media outlets? I'll tell them the same thing," I said.

Their faces lit up, and one of them began drafting an email on their laptop.

"What do you want to say?"

"Tell them that current afterlife status is unaffected assuming that one did not assist the State while they pursued me. Exact values are still being reevaluated, but if one

230

assisted in the revolution, they should expect to be rewarded in the next world."

The elevator slid open behind me, and Edward stepped out.

"Oh good, you saw your uniform. Looks pretty good, huh?" he asked me.

I thanked him for my uniform and directed his attention to the broadcast.

"Listen, Edward, do you think you can get me in front of a national audience? I want to deliver a televised message to the masses. They're worried about their afterlife status, and Vexrus and I both know how important it is for them to have that peace of mind. Besides, it's been a long night; I'm sure they could use an address from their leader."

"I think that can be arranged. We can probably set up a secure filming location at a loyalist local station by midafternoon, and we'll send the footage off to national stations right after."

"That would be perfect, thank you."

Edward smiled and left to prepare.

Visryan was repairing itself. The people wanted an afterlife system that guaranteed their ascension, and whatever deity they concocted would provide it for them. I looked around the room at my legion of competent, loyal subordinates. I was as much a cog in the machine as they were. I just enjoyed a particularly opulent position within it. Theocracies can't function without at least one unfaithful person.

Someone had to pull the strings that made god dance from the beginning. Without that all important centerpiece, the nation would cannibalize itself searching for meaning in a world where there was none. I didn't have complete control, however. I had to make god behave in such a way that the people found acceptable, lest someone else lose their faith and ascend to my status. When I was faithful, I thought that Vexrus could justify any action the State undertook, but when the State turned against me, I turned against Him. I had to give them a steady drip of reassuring rhetoric. Too much and the populous would become unproductive or even suicidal, depriving the State of much-needed workers and leading society to ruin. Too little and they would be buried under their own misery. Vexrus was both the carrot and the stick. I held both, but the overuse of either would make the people turn on me with their god behind them.

Media coverage became gradually more positive as the day wore on. One broadcast featured a member of the Supreme Council turning on his colleagues. Evidently, a few of them had read the writing on the wall and argued for me to become the fully legitimized ruler. The ever-growing hordes of Vexrus Firsters surrounding the capitol nudged the debate in our favor. If they failed to coronate me as emperor within the next day or so, they would likely be torn to shreds on the steps of the senate chamber. One particularly popular video circulating online showed a senior member of the Supreme Council calling me "the Monarch of Visryan."

I had yet to decide their fate. Their eagerness to switch sides only after the Vexrus First movement had taken power showed that they lacked faith and were willing to cede their political capital to me. I thought it safer to purge all non-believers, but having loyalists with intimate knowledge of Visryan's civil institutions would be invaluable. I ultimately decided to let the Supreme Council devour itself until a later date when I would choose who was to be executed and who was to become a de facto oligarch.

Riots in areas controlled by the Vexrus First movement died down while those in the few remaining State-loyal areas grew exponentially. The upper echelon of the Vexrus First movement began allocating more resources to these areas as our cache of seized weaponry grew. One media outlet prominently featured footage of their former rival's CEO being gunned down by a firing squad to illustrate their unwavering support.

Across the nation, Vexrus First flags replaced Visryan ones. Towns that once prided themselves on being home to members of the Supreme Council or Scholars defaced the monuments they had built to honor them. I asked every Vexrus Firster who showed up over the course of the day if they had seen any relevant dissenting demonstrations while they were out in town, and none had. Gradually, the consensus among the Supreme Council shifted in our favor as anti-Vexrus First members began to vanish. Statist media, what little remained of it, lamented the destruction of their nation as my supporters stormed into their studios. By midafternoon, *our* narrative became the only narrative. The organizations that had commanded citizens to maintain their loyalty now preached of a hopeful new era, one where the vile threat of the usurpers in the shadows would no longer pervert god's message. Visryan had fallen, and I alone knew why.

Chapter 20

Just before dusk, Edward brought me to a studio staffed with easily twice as much security as any Vexrus Study Institute. It was a small, local media outlet, one not accustomed to hosting important State announcements. The workers were thoroughly searched before they were allowed to enter the same room as me. I appreciated the security measure but doubted that it was necessary. The owner of the outlet lavished me with nonstop praise. I had eliminated his competition and chosen his company to broadcast my message. He had thrown his lot in with me wholeheartedly whether he believed in me or not.

I stood at a podium in front of the Vexrus First movement's, now Visryan's, flag, and addressed my legion of followers. I looked professional, like someone with the divine authority I claimed to have. Before the camera switched on, I ran my fingers across my shiny gold buttons and the insignia on my chest. I was a fabrication, a frightened fraud trying to survive another day, month, year. My only goal was to push the con forward. The faith of the nation rested on my heretical shoulders. I wondered if this was how the Scholars felt when they stood in front of the nation. I would have liked to speak with another Scholar or two before I had them killed, but of course, doing so would have been far too dangerous. I was alone now. As far as I knew, I was the only person in the entire country who knew of Vexrus' non-existence, and I would never tell a soul. I stood on top of a world superpower supported by a nation of bloodthirsty zealots. The ecstatic masses saw me on their television screens and believed that they were witnessing something cosmically significant. I alone feared death. I alone knew how hollow, meaningless, and temporary my revolution had been. Only I saw the rotting corpses laying in the gutter or the smoldering ruins of a once-functioning society or the people I had stepped on. Everyone else saw success; they saw a new world free of the fictitious oppression they had only been aware of for a couple of weeks. They saw liberation from monsters I had conjured from the ether.

"Are you ready, Mr. Wilson?" a cheery camerawoman said.

She had a Vexrus First movement pin on her chest, as did most of her co-workers.

"Yes, thank you, and do the other networks have access to this footage?" I asked.

"Everything is set up. The other friendly networks are instructing their audiences to tune in the moment they receive the recording. Your supporters are excited to see you," Edward said from just off screen.

I smiled and a little red light on the corner of the camera lit up.

"Greetings people of Visryan. Many of you have not seen me speak since the trial. Let me start my assuring you that I am unharmed and have exceptional security thanks to the former members of the Department of the Interior. I am sorry that the State has forced such hardship upon you. Let me assure you that Vexrus is a kind, just god. He wants nothing less than to see His adherents dying against a corrupt government. This unfortunate state of affairs has shown the weakness of the old Visryan. Evil grew within our own borders undetected. This is unacceptable! The watchful eye of the omnibenevolent State must be turned inward. We cannot be the pious nation we strive to be while suffering under the heel of our own officials. That's why, under my leadership, we will institute the most comprehensive surveillance operation in the nation's history, led by individuals handpicked by god. My administration will erect a city upon a hill, a nation that heathen foreigners will look at with envy, one free of parasitic non-believers. In order to accomplish this goal, it is important for each and every one of you to report instances of heretical thought to Vexrus First officials. The purge only ends when every heretic has been punished for their crimes. Your neighbors could be heretics, your family, the people teaching your children. Only with the aid of a vigilant populace can our great nation thrive. Join me, and make our nation a safe, moral, and proud place to raise the next generation. Remember, only a heretic has reason to fear the purge."

These security measures were crucial to the State's success. How could we risk even a single heretical thought penetrating the halls of academia? How could we allow the mumblings of possible heretics sitting at a bar to go unheard? Even with my divine right to rule, I needed to cast a wider net than the State was capable of casting. The citizenry had to become my eyes and ears. These heretical parasites wriggling their way into Visryan's civil institutions could hide from me, at least some of them could, but they could not avoid the critical gaze of their neighbor watching them through a crack in the wall. Those decrying my message weren't attacking me; they were attacking Vexrus and His people. My supporters needed to believe as dogmatically as I once had. Satisfied that I had trained my attack dogs, I moved on to the other aspect of theocratic governance: the afterlife.

"It has come to my attention that many of you are concerned about your afterlife status. Let me assure you that Vexrus cares about your loyalty first and foremost. Those of you that assisted the Vexrus First movement during our rise can expect to be rewarded, but those of you who stood with the State are encouraged to work your debt off as soon as possible. If you are a member of the latter group, there will soon be a way to report your failings to the State and receive an estimate for how you can be forgiven. If you have afterlife credits, you will keep them, assuming that you committed no egregious sins during the revolution. We will soon generate exact values for various transgressions and pious actions, but this will take some time."

Part of me enjoyed pulling strings through the television screen. A loyal statist in some isolated cabin somewhere was trembling at the thought of losing eternity. They thought that they were being a good citizen by standing with the State. They didn't know that I was legitimately god's elect. How could they have? Now they felt miserable. Now, they hated themselves for not recognizing my ascendent status sooner and would do anything to remedy this sin. Conversely, those who stood with the Vexrus First movement felt vindicated. I gave them a burst of dopamine that they would confuse for divine peace.

"Vexrus would like to award those who have demonstrated exceptional loyalty during this difficult time. Captain Eleanor Riley and Commander Edward Johansen are awarded guaranteed entrance to the afterlife, as well as anyone who gave their lives fighting against corrupted State forces."

I looked over at Edward who choked back tears. He mouthed "thank you" to me and received congratulatory handshakes from his subordinates. It cost me nothing to grant him this profound peace, but in exchange for it he would have given his life.

"Others will likely be given such an honor in the coming days. Vexrus tested this nation and its people, and we passed. To those who stand with me, Vexrus, and the Vexrus First movement, know this: eternity is yours. And to those who seek to destroy me and our god, you will face judgment," I said and motioned for the camera to be shut off.

I could hear crowds roaring outside after I finished. I had turned Visryan into a machine centered on my survival. If anyone realized the truth, sharing it would be a death sentence. My people would once again proudly march themselves into oblivion for a manufactured god. They had lost their theocracy once. Now, they would follow whatever order was necessary to maintain it.

Shortly after the speech, Edward cleaned out his office at the Department of the Interior Relis Headquarters and submitted recommendations for his replacement. Then, in full military regalia, Edward, having completed every task Vexrus had ever asked of him, rewarded himself for his hard work by hanging himself from a ceiling fan.

A few weeks later, long after the fires had died out and the last vestiges state influence had been erased, I, for the first time in months, felt safe and secure. A third or so of the Supreme Council remained, every one of them fiercely loyal and eager to prove themselves more pious than their colleagues. A few representatives, likely in an attempt at flattery, recommended that I hold a ceremony to celebrate the birth of a new Visryan and the crowning of the nation's first monarch. I agreed and, at least outwardly, the Supreme Council was elated. It was decided that we would hold it at the Capitol in the Senate chamber as a gesture of goodwill between the Supreme Council and the *new* highest authority in the land.

I rode in an armored limousine through throngs of faithful supporters. One woman fainted as I waived to her. Eleanor sat at my side clad in a new uniform emblazoned with her job title: Vicars' Guard Commander. Vexrus First movement banners hung from the roof of the capitol, and dozens of Eleanor's subordinates lined the stairs on either side. After a security update from Jessica, who had recently been made a lieutenant, I exited my vehicle to a chorus of thunderous applause. The remaining Council members stood at the top of the stairs waiting for me. I studied their faces; they lacked the jubilation of the onlookers. I operated under the assumption that every one of these men knew of Vexrus' nonexistence. The ceremony was an act for those involved, but not for the young Visryans who would be inspired by my ascension, or the up-and-coming media personality that needed their loyalty refreshed, or the still-conflicted would-be statist struggling to reconcile the world they had known with the revolution they had witnessed.

Eleanor ordered a pair of burly subordinates to open the door for me as I approached the top of the stairs. The

Council members filed in before me and took their positions on either side of a long red carpet embroidered with gold. At the far end sat a throne that, until my takeover, had been a decorative piece. It was meant to symbolize Vexrus' presence in the halls of power. Even when fallible human beings debated policy issues, the presence of the divine watched over them, ostensibly inspiring quality decision making. No one had ever sat in it before. After all, it was meant to be an unfillable seat. No mere man could sit on god's throne, but His chosen vicar could. I sauntered between the rows of Council members. As I passed, each one put their hand over their chest and took a knee, swearing their never-ending allegiance to Vexrus and His chosen mouthpiece.

I stopped at the end of the carpet and looked back over my shoulder at the Council members bending their knees. Some of the older ones struggled to maintain their pose, but they would not dare stand before being given permission. I ran my fingers along the iconography etched into the throne. It was covered in gaudy glistening gold. One Council member holding a mantle with art depicting Vexrus appearing before a nonbeliever on it approached me as I inspected it. I understood the meaning of this ritual; it was the same hurdle judges had to jump over: a symbolic gesture of subservience to Vexrus. He held it out in front of him and glanced at the ground, presumably expecting me to kneel.

I had no intention of presenting myself as anything short of divine. The State failed because it allowed me to separate it from god; I would make no such mistake. I took the cloak from him and wrapped it around myself, then glared at him until he knelt. Before the week was over, this man would stand in front of a firing squad. I sat on the throne and looked at the country I had ravaged and rebuilt. My will be done.

Hayden Hart studied English, Creative Writing, and Communications at Mercer University, and was a finalist for the 2020 Agnes Scott Writer's Festival Contest and other writing competitions. He enjoys speculative and dystopian fiction, which allows him to play with imaginative social structures and political or cultural systems.

www.ingramcontent.com/pod-product-compliance
Lightning Source LLC
La Vergne TN
LVHW090039090426
835510LV00038B/650